Talking the Talk About Autism

TaLKinG the TaLK About AutiSM

HOW to Share and tell your story

Haley MOSS

Jessica Kingsley Publishers
London and Philadelphia

First published in Great Britain in 2025 by Jessica Kingsley Publishers
An imprint of John Murray Press

1

A CIP catalogue record for this title is available from the
British Library and the Library of Congress

ISBN 978 1 83997 856 2
eISBN 978 1 83997 857 9

Printed and bound in the United States by Integrated Books International

Jessica Kingsley Publishers' policy is to use papers that are natural,
renewable and recyclable products and made from wood grown in
sustainable forests. The logging and manufacturing processes are expected
to conform to the environmental regulations of the country of origin.

Jessica Kingsley Publishers
Carmelite House
50 Victoria Embankment
London EC4Y 0DZ

www.jkp.com

John Murray Press
Part of Hodder & Stoughton Ltd
An Hachette Company

Contents

Acknowledgments

A BOOK LIKE THIS is impossible to write without the guidance, support, and love of an entire community—my own personal village. Writing a book is a huge undertaking, no matter how many times you set out to do it. It is a personal and professional sacrifice of time. It is a labor of love. It is no easy feat, but the people around you make the process all the more worthwhile and rewarding.

First off, to my parents, Sherry and Rick Moss. Also, the topic of this book would be out of the question without your unwavering support, guidance, and advocacy all of the years. I swear, I think you are geniuses for the ways you've managed to empower me and instill confidence within me since I was a little girl. "Thank you" is wholly inadequate. I love you so very much and am, as always, in awe of you and all you have done for me.

To the rest of our small but mighty family—Aunt Sandy and Uncle Sam, Aunt Cathy and Uncle Scott, my grandfather Howard, my other Aunt Sandy—thank you as well for always being by my side. I love you all!

To you, the reader—thank you for putting your trust and

time into this book, and for having an open heart and open mind to hearing my advice, regardless of what you do with it. Change is a magical, inspiring thing. I don't say that lightly. By listening to the voices of autistic people, you are choosing to be a changemaker in either your life or somebody else's, and for that, I am eternally grateful.

Introduction

I REMEMBER WHAT WAS POSSIBLY the first time I chose to tell somebody I was autistic. I chose someone who was a friend when I was 12 years old. My story up to that point was relatively simple (to me, at least)—I was diagnosed at three, my parents told me at nine, and here I was at 12 ready to tell a friend in hushed whispers while I was in the seventh grade. I was at my second school in two years and would eventually be on my way to a third in search of academic rigor to better fuel my curiosity and keep me from becoming too bored. I made very few friends, and the ones I did were also new kids or ones who were also different in some way, shape, or form.

I can't remember whether or not we were talking on the phone that night or if it was when we had a sleepover, but I remember telling this friend of mine, "I have autism." I was afraid, excited, and ashamed all at once. I didn't have the deep knowledge I do now, nor had I really begun the long journey of figuring out exactly what that meant to me. As a young adolescent, it meant I was not good at making friends, I misunderstood people and they also misunderstood me, I was honest to a fault and also different and creative. I had known this about myself for only three years. My autism was something I talked about with my family and my teachers to make sure I had opportunities to succeed. Telling my friend felt like telling her a scandalous secret, ripe for the middle school gossip mill, but she promised not to tell anyone. I immediately felt a pang of guilt for sharing, given this was something I intended to keep incredibly private and share only on a need-to-know basis. To me at the time, knowledge of my autism diagnosis would be reserved for family, teachers, healthcare team members, maybe my boss at a job, and/or a serious romantic partner.

My life has changed drastically since I was a 12-year-old who didn't know whether she was afraid, ashamed, or excited to talk about her autism. I have learned more about myself and autism than I could've ever imagined at that age. A year later, I was onstage at a conference telling an entire room of parents, self-advocates, and professionals about my journey and what being autistic meant to me. Later that summer, I began writing about my experiences and became an author at 15. You can Google my name and find out I am autistic. It is no longer the great big secret I had anticipated it would be when I was a young teenager.

My relationship with the autism community and autistic identity has morphed and changed drastically. As an author, I have to revisit my old work quite a bit. Sometimes, I feel proud of how I described my experiences and my community. Other times, I cringe and wish I had known then what I know now. I am much more confident overall, more self-assured, and I feel an awful lot less pressure to fit in and conform. *So what if they don't like me because I'm autistic*, I think.

Still, I talk about my autism nearly every day and some-times still have the same nervousness I did as a young person about how people around me will react, whether I'm saying too much or too little, if my language is accurate. As an advocate, I regularly have to be mindful of my wording—am I talking just about my individual experience, or things more universal to autistic culture and common characteristics and traits?

I get asked most times when I lead a workshop or via email from self-advocates, family members, and employers and colleagues alike, all about telling other people about their disability status. It is a question that has no singular, perfect answer. There is no formula to determine when is the "right" time, or that if you say a specific form of words, your conversation partner will have what you consider a perfect reaction of support, joy, or nonjudgment.

While I do not claim to have all the answers, I hope to give you some guidance as we work together to untangle the beautiful, complicated mess that is disclosure and talking about autism (and neurodiversity and disability as a whole).

In solidarity,
Haley

CHAPTER 1

How Exactly Do We Talk About Autism?

I HAVE A HABIT I need to break whenever I talk about autism: I assume people already know what autism is. It's a reasonable guess sometimes, given that in the United States, the Centers for Disease Control and Prevention estimate about 1 in 36 children today is identified as having an autism spectrum disorder (Centers for Disease Control and Prevention, 2023). By that estimate, chances are that you or somebody you know is autistic. In addition to encountering autism within our personal and professional lives, we have so much (albeit mixed) media representation of autism that is explicit, such as *Rain Man*, *Extraordinary Attorney Woo*, or *Atypical*, or perhaps more subtly coded, leaving viewers to interpret autistic traits within characters, like *The Queen's Gambit*, *Wednesday*, or *Lilo & Stitch*. Typically, if I mention "autism" to somebody less informed on the topic, their first comment is likely that they know an autistic person—a family member, a friend, a character—and then something about them (such as "I know what autism is, like the movie *Rain Man*!"). There's a lot to unpack there in terms of how I would respond; if I don't know the person well and it's casual, I might quietly nod and be like "Yeah, except that's not what it's like for me," and maybe share a detail or two; if it's someone I know well, we might have a much deeper conversation about media representation (*Rain Man* can be annoying) and my experiences. More informed people ask fewer questions or deeper questions about my struggles, or make a comment such as "I never would have known if you didn't tell me."

But sometimes, especially when I am around young people, they genuinely have no clue what autism is or is not. There's no all-encapsulating definition of autism that covers its nuances, individuality, or even the intersectional elements of how an autistic experience is influenced by race, gender, religion, sexuality, and so much more. The only consensus I can usually come to sharing is that autism is a neurodevelopmental disability, meaning it's brain-based, and different traits show up when a toddler or kid is growing up. People don't acquire autism, though they might discover they were always autistic all along and have a name for their experiences through a self-identification or a late diagnosis. Finding the right words to use for everyone's level of understanding or development can prove to be a tricky task.

What also makes autism so complicated is an old saying within the autism community. Dr. Stephen Shore, a professor at Adelphi University, is often quoted as saying, "If you've met one person with autism, you've met one person with autism"—effectively, no two people on the spectrum are the same or share the exact same constellation of behaviors and traits. For instance, I am a very picky eater who eats the same few foods, yet I have autistic friends who will try every special that is on a restaurant menu. Sometimes I can make eye contact, albeit not very well, while others exclusively look off into space or at the floor.

How I define autism

As a very literal person, I decided to do some homework to help us come up with a good definition to make sure we're on the same page. Nobody has a consistent definition of autism. A lot of the times I speak with well-meaning folks who want to learn, they have a plethora of questions or struggle to associate my experiences with somebody else's they know, circling back to that "if you know one person with autism, you know one person with autism" mindset.

The Diagnostical and Statistical Manual of Mental Disorders (DSM-5; APA, 2013) says autistic people must have deficits in social-emotional reciprocity, nonverbal communicative behaviors, and developing, maintaining, and understanding relationships, in addition to meeting other criteria for stereotypical or repetitive motor movements, insistence on sameness/routine, highly fixated special interests, or sensory issues. Honestly, going through autism as a checklist like this and grading the "severity" of each of these things to account for the spectrum can be confusing and approaches autism from a deficit-based understanding, which makes me feel a bit uneasy.

That's a huge contrast to the Autistic Self-Advocacy Network's definitions, which acknowledge how there's no one way to be autistic, but some common experiences are how we think, process senses, move, communicate, and socialize differently, and may need help with daily living (Autistic Self Advocacy Network 2024). I really like this, and their website describes each of these things with a lot more detail, but sometimes it doesn't do the trick given how autism can be (for many, myself included) disabling at the same time. It's a difficult balance to strike.

Usually, I try to blend these two schools of thoughts together into one cohesive definition. Here's the best I came up with:

> Autism is a complex neurological condition and developmental disability characterized by a spectrum of differences in social communication and interaction, heightened sensory processing and experiences, intense passions or interests, and repetitive behaviors.

From there, I might choose to focus on or explain the things most relevant to me, like how some of those communication differences may be that I miss sarcasm or other seemingly innate social cues, that I have an aversion to very loud noises or bright spaces, what my current passions are, and how my body moves and I fidget and whatnot to stay calm. This helps humanize and put people at ease since there are an awful lot of terms that might not make sense right away to the average person.

However, you might want to blend some of these things together depending on who you're talking to about autism and their level of knowledge. For instance, children do not have the same vocabulary or level of understanding as adults, but are very open-minded and can practice acceptance with ease. With little kids, I might say something like:

> For me, autism is a disability that makes the world feel very loud and scary sometimes, and I don't always understand why

people say and do the things they do, so it can be hard to make friends, and sometimes my body moves in ways your body might not.

This explains sensory sensitivities, social differences, and stimming behavior in a way anybody can understand, and the "for me" at the beginning helps make it clear that might not be the same experience someone else has (maybe for you, autism is less sensory, but you also have an intellectual disability or use augmentative and alternative communication, like typing or sign language, also known as "AAC").

As the scientific community learns more about autism's roots and values autistic experiences more, and the autistic community grows in size, I'm certain our definition of autism might change on a broader scale. But for now, I'm adapting with the information we have available to us and based on who I'm speaking with.

My interpretation and how I define autism have also changed the older I get. I am not a nonspeaking autistic toddler anymore. I am no longer a late talker who primarily used echolalia until I was about six years old. As a teenager, I might have downplayed how perhaps autism made me feel socially out of touch or awkward, but now there are things I have names for that I didn't back then. How I stim has changed; the happy, excited flapping hands only come out on occasions of sheer joy that my body cannot contain otherwise. My passions and special interests have evolved alongside me, going from Ancient Egypt to Harry Potter to shopping and other things, but the arts, Pokémon, and video games have always been fairly consistent sources of autistic joy for me. My sensory issues largely haven't changed, except that the advocacy tools

I have to get out of uncomfortable situations have certainly gotten better.

So now, when I have to talk about my own autism with other adults, I am a lot more focused, a lot more honest, a lot more aware. I talk about how my biggest adult challenge is executive functioning due to my inability to stay focused on something that doesn't interest me, my lack of ability to keep track of time, prioritize, start and stop tasks, and remember to do silly little things that I am pretty sure most people think of as "stuff their parents nagged them to do as kids or teenagers" (cleaning my room, remembering to put my retainers in my mouth before bedtime). Usually, these specific instances of my autism are relatable enough for allies and non-autistic people to understand since they are typical struggles with a few distinguishing features; I do want to clean my apartment but the sheer number of steps can make it super overwhelming, which is why I've even written about how to break it down in *The Young Autistic Adult's Independence Handbook*. I'll talk about the differences in socialization and how it often feels as though I am a second-language learner doing my best to speak "neurotypical" when not a lot of people will adapt to try to speak my native language or learn a few handy phrases or guiding principles for neurodivergent or autistic communication. Instead, they criticize me for not speaking the neurotypical social language perfectly.

Unpacking ableism

I have to admit—even though this book is about disclosure, it's really also a reflection about identity. How we view ourselves and what we know about our own neurodivergence is also part of how we share our own identities, tell our stories, and advocate for ourselves. It is never a perfectly smooth road, and my journey with autistic identity has been a rollercoaster, to put it lightly. I began advocating publicly in my early teens, and am likely going to be in my 30s by the time you are reading this. Needless to say, so much has changed in the close to two decades I have been involved in autism advocacy.

The way I have felt about my own autism has changed greatly since my early teens. In my teenage years, I didn't know many other autistic people, and I internalized a lot of stigma, stereotypes, and beliefs about autism. I thought my experience was unique and singular in the fact that I didn't know other autistics in my school, social circle, or life. The people I did know were largely nonspeaking and had intellectual disabilities, and I thought I had little in common with them (I was very wrong). I clung to my "high-functioning" diagnosis.

As I look back on some of my writing and work, I realize that I had at times been passing on my own ableism and internalized beliefs about my disability status. Learning about and naming ableism for what it is helps me be a better advocate and ally, and avoid passing on harmful, offensive, and often outdated beliefs—and gives all of us a better opportunity to make interactions go smoothly and enable us to receive and give support to one another.

What's the deal with ableism?

For a very long time, I remember insisting on the many ways I wanted to be treated just like everybody else. I wanted to be invited to sleepovers, birthday parties, and playdates as a kid because someone actually would want to hang out with me. When I was in high school, I went to our school's college fair, where all the universities were advertising their programs and student life, and a classmate of mine told me I wouldn't have to worry about admission to those schools because "You have a disability. You could've been born a vegetable. Colleges love that stuff"—and it made me wonder if I was somehow being pitied and had it easier despite the fact that I was taking the same classes and trying to have a well-balanced array of extracurricular activities just like my neurotypical peers did. Later on, I wanted to have a "typical college experience" and requested to have a roommate rather than take advantage of a single living arrangement offered to me that would be better suited to my needs (I ended up doing that once the "typical roommate experience" was not working well for me) because I didn't want to be viewed as different. At work, I had been offered accommodations I didn't want or need or advocate for; meanwhile, years prior, when I entered law school, I was denied accommodations because I wasn't "disabled enough" and my peers thought I had an unfair advantage due to the assumption that I received every accommodation possible.

All of these experiences have one thread in common—they are instances where I've experienced *ableism* in its many flavors. Simply put, ableism really speaks to the biases, discrimination, and prejudice that negatively impact people with disabilities.

Ableism is also a bit more complicated than that too. The Center for Disability Rights (n.d.) explains:

Ableism is a set of beliefs or practices that devalue and dis-criminate against people with disabilities and often rests on the assumption that disabled people need to be "fixed" in one form or the other. Ableism is intertwined in our culture, due to many limiting beliefs about what disability does or does not mean, how able-bodied people learn to treat people with disabilities and how we are often not included at the table for key decisions.

This to me is where things get interesting. For autistic people, that external belief from society about being "fixed" relates inherently to the disclosure conversations we're having throughout this book. A literal "fixing" takes us to the idea that many autistic people do not want a cure for autism, whereas others expressly do, and there are many who just want science and improved, dedicated research and innovation to grant us some quality-of-life improvements without altering our neuro-types. Debates around "fixing" autistic people involve a variety of approaches, from therapies and interventions, to a societal focus on replacing autistic social skills with neurotypical ones, to wild speculating about causes of autism and other potential scientific discoveries or theories.

However, the assumption that we are failed versions of nor-mal needing to be "fixed" to be more neurotypical isn't always as obvious or medical-sounding in nature. A more abstract version of being "fixed" is how some (but not all) autistic people may feel an inherent societal and cultural pressure to be "normal" and rely heavily on masking and camouflaging strategies to suppress autistic traits like stimming or talking at length about special interests, or they play up certain neu-rotypical social skills like eye contact and script reactions and conversations, to avoid ableism, exclusion, bullying, and more. While it was initially believed that masking is solely inherent to girls and women, masking and camouflaging happen in all types of autistic people in order to survive and thrive in a neurotypical world; our motivations for these survival strategies differ depending on the circumstances around us and the identities we hold. For instance, girls and women may mask so that they can navigate friendships and school environments, or keep themselves safe from sexual harassment and assault; autistic people of color may mask and suppress stims and other autistic traits in order to avoid suspicion from law enforcement and racial profiling in addition to disability discrimination. Regardless of the motivation, masking is tough and has plenty of adverse effects on autistic people, including but not limited to burnout, depression, anxiety, low self-esteem, and internalized ableism. It also feeds into many conversations and decisions a person may make surrounding disclosure.

A lot of well-intentioned allies also engage in ableism because of their *limiting beliefs about what disability does or does not mean*. Disability covers an awful lot of identities, bodies, and brains. Autism also is a diverse spectrum with varying traits, and people of different races, genders, ages, sexual orientations, and more. So often, one of those wrinkles of ableism I encounter is when people will assume I am "high-functioning" and will give me more respect than non-speakers or autistics with intellectual disabilities. Another version of this is when folks comment that they never would have known that I was autistic if I didn't tell them, or that I can't possibly be autistic because I am talkative and a woman. When I am passing or indistinguishable from neurotypicals, I recognize it's a result of years of learning the neurotypical social language as well as masking.

This also spirals into *how neurotypical, nondisabled people learn to treat neurodivergent people*. Ableism is partly why I struggle with navigating the world at times. If I am masking heavily or appear socially competent, I am treated with a lot more respect compared to when I might appear more visibly autistic—when I am overwhelmed from a sensory overload, feel immense empathy and intense emotions, don't react the "correct" way, or am stimming or fidgeting. When it comes to autism, new people I meet genuinely do not know how to act or treat me upon learning about my disability. I have been assumed to have an intellectual disability as well as being autistic, so people will sometimes speak more slowly to me or assume I no longer understand things even if we were having a deep conversation. Well-meaning folks might also talk down to me or offer unsolicited advice based on their experiences with another autistic person they know. Other times, people's curiosity makes them feel entitled to know all sorts of personal or sensitive information about me based on disability; total strangers may want to know about standardized test scores, my sex life, the depths of my medical history, complete with what doctors and prescription medications may or may not be a part of my life (which is information that should primarily always be between a person and their healthcare team, not up for discussion with someone you've never met before to satisfy their curiosity or desperate search for information). Sometimes, they know to treat me like anybody else (the best outcome) while also being mindful and respectful of my needs when I advocate for myself. It's tough navigating my desire to be treated similarly to my peers and have my competence presumed, while also feeling understood and validated in what makes me unique and where I may need additional support. Generally, in unlearning my own bias, I try to assume everyone understands me unless they give me a reason to believe or tell me otherwise—then I will speak more slowly, use plain language, provide extra time to process, or change how I interact with them. Assumptions generally aren't very helpful and can feed into bias.

Activist and scholar Talila "TL" Lewis has a more complicated working definition of ableism that annually evolves based on the needs of our communities. After all, everybody is impacted by ableist beliefs and practices. I am not absolved of ableism simply because I experience it; my life experience is a singular one and doesn't encompass the entire disabled community or a variety of different identities and diagnoses. According to Lewis, ableism places value and worthiness on certain bodies and minds depending on societal ideas of productivity, wellness, fitness, intelligence, normalcy, and desirability (Lewis, 2022). This is connected to other forms of oppression.

But one takeaway I appreciate from Lewis is that you do not have to be disabled to experience ableism. I like to point this out to family members of neurodivergent kids, who have likely felt ostracized or excluded because of their relative's diagnoses. These family members—often parents and siblings—may be told they are brave, receive fewer opportunities for inclusion in community programs and activities, experience less peer support, or are otherwise treated differently than other families *because* they have an autistic or disabled family member. I sometimes tell a story from a few years ago about spending time with a lawyer colleague who has cerebral palsy and is a wheelchair user; when we've been out at a restaurant, the waitstaff immediately asked me what my colleague would like to order, assuming I was their caregiver or sister. Meanwhile, we were both lawyers, and this person is perfectly capable of ordering their own food. I was being perceived as neurotypical and nondisabled; I shrugged and politely suggested speaking to my colleague instead. It was a very "outside looking in" experience for me the first time I was perceived as not having a disability while around others with more apparent disabilities, and it forced me to reflect on how being assumed to be a "good person" or "saint" as a caregiver or sibling is a form of bias, as well—when we're just doing the best we can as friends, family members, colleagues, and allies.

Finally, to wrap up, the Center for Disability Rights' definition of ableism is *how we are often not included at the table for key decisions.* This can be in our own lives or within the community. When I am asked what I need and want, it often looks very different from what other people assume I need or want. In school, the assumption was always that I would need extra time as the only accommodation presented to me as an option. However, I needed help with socialization, and when I got to college and law school, I would've likely benefited greatly from note-taking services because my ability to listen, write, and process information simultaneously isn't that great due to my autism and executive functioning challenges. As a young person, I didn't quite know this, nor was it presented as an option because the blanket assumption was that I needed extra time and I wouldn't be at the table for the decision. Our exclusion also calls to mind the disability rights phrase "Nothing about us without us."

Key decisions also relate to my goals. In many ways, the goals I have look a lot like those of my nondisabled peers. I want a career I enjoy, the love of my family and friends, to have a supportive and loving relationship to share with a life partner, a roof over my head in a place I like, and financial independence so that my family shouldn't have to worry about me in that regard. The order of importance of these is where people often go awry when making assumptions about me. It's assumed I might not want those deep interpersonal connections. Nor will people help me foster or make new friends and relationships, or nurture the ones I already have (somehow, a lot of effort disproportionately seems to fall on me when communication is a two-way street).

I often tell people to get involved in community organizations, nonprofits, and other disability rights and justice issues on the internet. So often, their boards of directors, decision makers, employees, donors, and volunteers are nondisabled people making decisions for us. One of the boards I have served on for an autism organization had admitted that they rarely, if ever, had autistic input in leadership, and it wasn't until I advocated that autistic members joined the board or had their voices heard among the other board members, mostly comprised of donors and parent-advocates. One admitted that in decades of existence, they never had autistic people on their board of directors who served in an elected leadership position like President, Vice President, Secretary, or Treasurer. Others have expressed frustration or apathy towards the people with disabilities they serve and employ due to disability-related characteristics and traits. I don't say any of this to diminish the important work of allies and family members—they are so crucial to inclusion and do a lot of amazing, necessary work—but theirs shouldn't be the *only* voices in the room, especially on autism or disability issues. It's a lot like those commercials you see on TV asking for money related to other health conditions, where you hear from the patients, doctors, researchers, and family members—except you don't often see or hear the stories from the autistic person directly, just everybody else around them.

The same goes for making key decisions in our own lives. At its most extreme is the population of adults within the American guardianship and conservatorship system. This legal tool is supposed to be one of last resort in order to give parents, caregivers, and professional guardians control and decision-making power in situations where a person with a disability is unable to make their own decisions or care for themselves, likely permanently. In the United States, studies have shown over half of young adults with intellectual and developmental disabilities aged 18 to 22 have a legal guardian and lose a wide variety of civil rights, meaning they are under another person's care and have restrictions and a lack of autonomy over choices such as where they can live and work, who provides care, who they may date or marry or if they may have families of their own, how they can manage their money or healthcare decisions. They even lose other rights such as the right to vote. In essence, another person or entity has complete control over your life and decision-making processes, and this can put autistic people in especially vulnerable and potentially abusive situations. Getting out of a guardianship can be near impossible, with a lengthy and expensive legal process (Moss, 2023). As the National Council on Disability explains, "guardianship orders impact the very decisions that define people as human beings, and thus have a significant impact on the daily lives of people subject to them" (National Council on Disability, 2018).

Less extreme than guardianship are the many ways our priorities and goals are often not the same as the ones our peers, family members, and professionals hold for us. If you ask me about my goals and dreams and priorities, they look awfully similar to those of my non-autistic, neurotypical peers. I want (and thankfully have) a career I find fulfilling and I feel a sense of purpose with my work. While I do live independently, I want someday to move to a house or apartment with an extra bedroom so I can have a separate, dedicated workspace rather than a desk in my bedroom or my kitchen table, as well as additional closets or storage space for my things. I want to have, hold, build, and nurture meaningful relationships in my life—be more ambitious about my friendships, maintain and grow the strong relationships I have within my family, and maybe someday have that special kind of enduring love and shared existence with a lifelong partner. None of these things mention or are related to disability challenges I face. It might have taken a little more support to find and create the right career path for me and I've had to learn the art of disclosure, advocating for accommodations, and finding accepting and passionate people to surround myself with, but that was not impossible due to a perceived inability of mine or autism itself closing the door on opportunity (if anything, other people are the ones who close doors rather than open them). Many of my peers also want to move to another place to experience somewhere new, need more space like I do, or have families of their own. And, of course, many people crave and want love in their lives, though, like anyone and anything, it requires patience, the right time and place, and a person who is accepting and understanding, and who shares similar values and morals. However, the order of these priorities might be different, and it's important to talk to somebody on the spectrum about their priorities; like everybody else, those priorities can change and shift. Finishing my education and building my career were the top priorities for me in my early twenties, more so than "living independently" (which is almost always touted as the top goal for young adults with disabilities—I mostly lived at my parents' home during the pandemic, and none of us viewed it as some kind of failing at an "independence goal"). Now, one of my top goals is full financial independence to ensure my family does not have to worry about me, though sometimes their top goal for me might look a little different or be one of my other goals. I know my family will always support my goals and endeavors, no matter what, but having those raw, honest conversations and allowing us to take the driver's seat in our own lives in establishing goals and priorities—and having action plans to achieve (and backup plans if they seem inaccessible at the moment)—should take precedence over what the "perceived" perfect goal based on autism or disability *should* be.

Being excluded from the halls of power or decision making in our own lives makes others believe we are helpless or unable to make our own decisions or advocate for ourselves. Instead, the efforts should go into making sure we're empowered to advocate for ourselves, and others to advocate *with* us, and not always *for* us. That small distinction of linking up together to move the needle of inclusion further makes all the difference.

The sneakiest of them all: benevolent ableism

With disclosure, the subtype of ableism I really want to highlight is *benevolent ableism*. Benevolent ableism occurs when people—allies in particular—act with good intentions but make assumptions that end up hurting someone's feelings, denying someone's independence, or impinging on their ability to make their own decisions. People with disabilities historically often receive and are offered various forms of assistance that are neither wanted nor needed. It ends up making us feel helpless, or as though we aren't trusted to make key decisions for ourselves.

Here is a key example from my lived experience that I share with allies, when I experienced benevolent ableism, mostly rooted in social exclusion. When I was at the end of my eighth-grade year, I had a very good friend. I had previously been to her house for a sleepover and was familiar with (but not super close with) her other friends at school since we'd all spent time socializing together outside of school in an effort to include me since I was the new kid at school that year, too. When her birthday was approaching, she was hosting the entire friend group on a trip to Disney World. I was the only one who was not invited. I knew this trip was approaching because it was all anybody could talk about—I knew how excited the other girls were, planning what attractions they'd visit at the Disney parks and what outfits they would wear. When the trip came and went by, my hurt at exclusion only grew because I saw all the photos and updates in real time on Facebook. Knowing this was coming, my family and I had spoken extensively about the trip and my mom even spoke to my friend's parents about my exclusion. We quickly pieced together that I likely was excluded because I was autistic—my friend's parents assumed if I went on the trip, it would be too much for them to handle, and I wouldn't want to go because a theme park with a group of girls may have been too socially advanced for me. Rest assured, though: we were told numerous times about how my friend deeply cared about me. Had I been invited; my family and I could've talked through our options for my inclusion and accessibility concerns if I even wanted to join the group on the trip. The sting of exclusion under the guise of caring about me only made the situation worse than if my friend didn't even like me or want me there in the first place.

Upon reflection, this type of social exclusion and benevolent ableism is actually a form of bullying—something my own ableism did not allow me to recognize as a younger person, because I thought bullying was mostly name-calling, physical cruelty like a punch, or spreading rumors. I never would have thought of my friends as bullies when they were single-handedly deciding what I would and would not want to participate in, since they were telling me they cared and had my best interests at heart. It is a very messy experience that spills over into my adult life today, where invitations to certain outings are not even offered because someone is "looking out for me" or doesn't think I will want to go somewhere loud and crowded or eat the food. Sure, it's often the case you won't find me lining up to join you at a bar, nightclub, networking event, or sushi restaurant, but there's a chance I will still agree to go for a short time just to catch up with you, or I'll try to go, even though I know it may be too much for me and I already looked at the menu and planned my "exit strategy" well before even showing up.

All of this is to say that benevolent ableism feels kind. It's not always easy to identify, but think about how often we want to be in charge of decisions. When looking to unlearn these polite, caring types of actions that end up excluding or assuming we know what someone needs or wants, think about how you might feel if someone doesn't ask about your preferences or desires. It can be hurtful. Keep in mind that this doesn't show up just in friendships and relationships. Benevolent ableism also shows up a lot in the workplace, and we will delve deeper into that when we talk about disclosure in professional settings. It is always well-meaning, and sometimes difficult to navigate and work through—but we'll learn how to figure out those tough situations as both self-advocates and allies alike.

Internalized ableism

The hardest one to navigate as an autistic person for me is *internalized ableism*. This is what happens when a person with a disability accepts the stereotypes and stigmas surrounding disability, such as believing they are "too much" for asking for help, feeling as though they need to "prove people wrong about disability" or that they are lazy and stupid when really their brain just works differently and processes information unlike their peers. Some thoughts we might have relating to internalized ableism are "I'm not good enough," "I will never get a job," "I am broken and need to be fixed," or "I am asking for too much" because of autism. Internalized ableism can impact our self-esteem, our self-concept as autistic or neurodivergent people, or even how we teach others to treat us and acknowledge our needs.

For me, internalized ableism is partly why I never felt comfortable asking for accommodations or help. I was always afraid I would be burdening someone else or putting them out with my request. Sometimes I'd be nervous I'd be looked down upon and treated worse for having a disability. I also had this belief for a long time that if I had asked for and needed more frequent assistance, I'd lose whatever independence I had (and this is something I investigated quite a bit in *The Young Autistic Adult's Independence Handbook*).

For me, internalized ableism looks like believing I might be burdening others if I ask for accommodations or if we go to a different restaurant for dinner because of my autism-related food aversions or the potential for a sensory overload. Sometimes it is believing I am lazy or unmotivated when I struggle with executive functioning tasks or that I am incredibly moody and difficult when I am just heavily dysregulated from a sensory and social perspective. For others, internalized ableism might be adapting coping strategies such as increased masking and camouflaging to attempt to appear more neurotypical or less autistic in order to gain acceptance and validation from others and within.

I also felt I had to "overcome" autism a lot because of internalized ableism. When I was in school, I felt immense internal pressure to "prove" that I deserved to take up the same space as anyone else. When I was a fresh-faced 21-year-old entering law school, a professor at orientation had the nerve to tell me right away I was occupying a seat in the graduating class that should belong to someone with more life experience than me. I thought this was due to age primarily, but I realized there was also an assumption about my disability and being naïve; there's a sort of stereotype about autistic and disabled people about how others might be "protecting" us from the world or we are sheltered into separate environments for school and employment. It was assumed I would only be interested in certain positions, and I wasn't given resources or tools to navigate disclosure and self-advocacy. Instead, the only way I was getting the same opportunities as my neurotypical, nondisabled peers was when I was overachieving. Not only was I taking the same classes, and earning similar grades, but I had to prove my competence by being incredibly involved with activities at school and outside of school (and then holding multiple leadership positions), other internship and work experience opportunities, and volunteering. I didn't want to be wrongly labeled as a lazy person with a disability or become another unemployment statistic, or be viewed as somehow letting my community down. I would juggle all of these obligations and be labeled as superwoman, but I felt exhausted from the competing demands for my time. The collection of honors and responsibilities caused employers and university admissions to view me as a competent, high achiever *despite my* disability, rather than someone who was perfectly capable in the same way my "average" peers were, and I had to somehow prove myself more, but at what personal cost? I am by no means trying to overcome autism; rather, I am trying to overcome society's barriers. I am also finally learning I can say yes to things because I want to, not because I have to prove a point or appear to be superhuman in order to command the same respect and human dignity as nondisabled, neurotypical peers.

Regardless, these types of behaviors and beliefs about autistic people can lead to all sorts of hard feelings throughout our lives, and it takes active work to unlearn the stigmatizing things we have been taught by others and our society. It isn't always easy, and internalized ableism is still something I struggle with quite a lot, but attitudes from others around us and naming these difficult emotions with vulnerability allow us to heal and grow.

The high-functioning and low-functioning trap

The older I get, the more conscious I become of my own biases. Growing up, I did not meet other autistic people, in an autistic space, until I was about 13 years old. I was in a mainstream, general education classroom and surrounded largely by neurotypical kids. As an only child, most of my interactions were with adults.

Needless to say, my frame of reference on autism was fairly limited. My first introduction to autism representation came from *The Baby-Sitters Club* book series in one particular installment titled *Kristy and the Secret of Susan*, where the babysitters were caring for an autistic girl named Susan during the summer. Susan was eight years old, largely nonspeaking, and diagnosed with what was then known as Rhett syndrome. She had savant abilities like a calendar in her head and was able to play pretty much any song from memory on the piano. I totally did not relate to her and learned some biases from my favorite book series. I thought I had nothing in common with this nonspeaking, savant girl. In reality, both of us faced exclusion from our own local communities and neighborhood kids and families. Our parents wanted us to have the best quality of life by any means possible and also felt like they could benefit from greater support and acceptance. But as an elementary school kid in the early 2000s, there is no way I was thinking like I do now; instead, all I was able to conceptualize was I was not receiving special education services or being sent away from home to go to another school; I was verbal, had a few real friends, and believed I was smart. I was, as the language suggested, "high-functioning."

As a young person, I clung desperately to the "high-functioning" label that came along with my diagnosis, something that distinguished me from kids like Susan. "Autistic, but not like that," was one of the connotations of being described as high-functioning; it created an artificial distance between me and folks I had way more in common with than I thought as a young person.

I learned throughout the years, and thanks to having a robust autistic community around me, that "high-functioning" and "low-functioning" end up being harmful—and also one of neurotypical people's first reactions if I talk to them about my autism ("you must be really high-functioning"). I never really knew how to respond to this reaction, but I've come to realize it makes me feel awkward and uncomfortable, even if it's well intended to say that my autism must not be as difficult on a daily basis as someone who may face more barriers than I do. Other people experience my autism more mildly than someone who needs ongoing care and daily support in the majority of things they do, but my experience doesn't negate the disabling nature of autism at times.

It's true that non-speakers or autistics with intellectual disabilities need different, if not more, support than I do. I am able to live on my own, hold a job, advocate for myself, and do a lot of things on my own or with limited input from others. Some people do need the help of a caregiver, may not be employed, and struggle to advocate for themselves or communicate. Every experience of autism is unique, and challenging, and wonderful, all at once. Since it is a spectrum, there are differences, but our similarities are what bring us together. When I look back at *The Baby-Sitters Club*, it turns out both Susan and I were struggling socially, and people were overtly or subtly excluding us or being mean behind our backs; we were both overwhelmed by our environments and had families who wanted the best for us in the face of ableism. How's that for something in common, even if our day-to-day realities were very different?

I don't like to grade humans based on functioning. When I was a college student, I remember reading a really smart blog post by Cynthia Kim on Musings of an Aspie, where she describes two separate people, Mary and Joan. It is supposed to be obvious which woman is "high-functioning" and which is "low-functioning." The twist was Mary and Joan are the same person created from Kim's own traits, just selected and highlighted separately (Kim, 2013). The lesson is how fluid and nonlinear functioning really is.

Applying this to my own life, I could tell you there is a version of me who is a lawyer, lives on her own, is very motivated, has friends, with hobbies like reading, writing, and watching sports (that would be the "high-functioning" part of this example), and there is another version of me who struggles to stay organized and tidy, has difficulty and becomes easily overwhelmed in social situations, startles from the sound her dryer makes when the laundry is done, can't park the car because of spatial awareness and driving brings on bouts of anxiety, and loves Disney, Pokémon, and video games (that would probably be the "low-functioning" part). But I am all of those things on any given day, and sometimes how much sleep I've had or how much my sensory system was overloaded will determine how pronounced certain traits are. I'm just human. My struggles and successes, like anybody else's, do not define my worth.

But really, when I'm faced with the commentary of high- and low-functioning today, I don't explain the nonlinear nature of it. It's probably too much for someone who meant well. If I have to explain, I say, "Thanks, but all people on the autism spectrum have a lot in common, like difficulties with communication and sensory stuff" to keep it light. If I'm explaining to someone I know better, I might explain that "high-functioning diminishes my needs and doesn't allow me to receive support, while low-functioning diminishes the potential and dignity of others." In other words, I've been told I am fine and don't need help when I do, and someone who needs more help than I do is told they can't do stuff.

Either way, try to approach the situation with grace and assume the best of intentions. I know for many of us, learning and unlearning biases and classifying people is difficult work. I've had to do it myself. It's one of the hardest forms of internalized ableism to work through, so please extend grace to yourself whenever possible.

Advocating for myself

One of the biggest biases and sources of internalized ableism that I am working really, really hard on is trying not to minimize things that are hard for me. When I minimize, it also ensures I don't receive proper support or I am just severely misunderstood. Sometimes, when I am very dysregulated from a routine or sensory perspective, I am more irritable and not quite myself. Instead of asking for help, I just kind of ride the wave until I'm able to escape a situation, and others then think I am simply very moody, when I should just ask for assistance or share that I am dysregulated or overwhelmed. I recognize this is a hard thing to do for me (and others) because we're afraid of judgment, a "no" answer, or being told some comment about how the real world is not always accommodating, so we have to merely accept this as a part of life.

Self-advocacy is difficult. We're expected to learn the ins and outs of using our voices and expressing our needs and wants almost flawlessly from a young age.

Even as a prospective and former neurodivergent law student, I was expected to have the advocacy skills and toolbox of an experienced lawyer or even a much more mature person than my younger self was. While it is presumed most students can advocate for themselves flawlessly once they reach adulthood and their caregivers, legal guardians, or other adults no longer are able to do it for them, that isn't always the case. Sometimes, it's extremely helpful to have someone else by your side to fill in the gaps or if you need support—especially if there's denial from the powers that be. Since I didn't always know how to navigate a system while I was in my undergraduate studies, I didn't even bother after a while and therefore went through law school without accommodations. I didn't know how to or whether it would be worth the energy to fight back. This circles around to ableism yet again—this belief that I, too, am less deserving perhaps of accommodations, that in the eyes of academia I was "not disabled enough" based on the documentation I had that spanned most of my life. Now, several years later, I am learning not to regret my decision to forgo accommodations in the face of an inaccessible disability services system, but to be kinder to my 21-year-old self, who was nervous, scared, living truly independently for the first time in her own apartment in a new city, and was starting rigorous education and training for a legal career. Now that I *do* have the skills I was expected to have, I recognize how unreasonable that may have been to expect of a young person, and I extend my younger self a lot more grace for not having those skills. So it's totally okay if your advocacy and disclosure skills are still in the works and vary greatly from situation to situation.

The advocacy and disclosure recap

Wow, that was a lot of information to get us started! To reflect and have some takeaways and reminders as you go through this book:

- Explaining disability, autism, and neurodiversity can feel tricky, but having definitions and examples to describe traits relevant to you or somebody else makes it a little bit easier. You might have to adjust your definitions and examples based on somebody else's age, maturity, and level of understanding, or even your comfort level.

- Ableism is everywhere, including within ourselves, and we don't always get it right. This is a pervasive form of bias where people with disabilities experience negative treatment, including stereotyping, stigma, and discrimination. Sometimes, we can even believe in these things and struggle with internalized ableism.

- If you are neurodivergent or disabled, your identity journey and relationship with disability can and will change as you learn more, mature, and create a healthier understanding and possibly a little bit more self-love. I began as a curious kid who thought she had superpowers and never met another autistic person in my life, and whose only frame of reference was an outdated one-off fictional character in a book series. Since my early teenage advocacy days, I've learned to ditch functioning labels, met a lot more autistic, neurodivergent, and disabled people, and have much more acceptance of my own strengths and challenges.

- A lot of us are thrown to the wolves, it seems, in having to advocate for ourselves and our needs, and a big piece of that is disclosure. It is incredibly hard to figure out the right time, place, and words to describe our experiences and make space for other people to assist us in order for us to thrive in our daily lives without our disability-related challenges taking center stage in whatever we do.

CHAPTER 2

Why Is Disclosure So Tricky?

E VERY TIME I MEET A NEW PERSON, I am immediately
wracking my brain trying to figure out how they are per-
ceiving me. *Do they think I'm nice? Funny? Smart? Awkward?
Am I fidgeting or is my body moving in a way that is different
from theirs? Am I talking too much?* Of course, it's natural to
want people to like us, but the way these things run through
my brain a million miles a minute could make anybody feel
self-conscious and possibly anxious. It means I have to confront
one question that looms over my other thoughts of how I'm
being interpreted and understood: *Do they know I am autistic?*

Whether or not someone knows I am autistic is very, very
context dependent. Sometimes I am quick to make sure they
know to diffuse any potential tension; other times I can go
without them ever knowing until one day I'm met with a
confused "Really?" type of reaction. If someone knows, it can
make things easier with understanding and acceptance, while
other times it can make it harder with more judgment and
follow-up questions.

At this point in my life, it is no secret that I am autistic—it's
interwoven into everything I do. I've been outspoken about

my autism for well over half of my time on this planet thus far. I even went viral back in 2019 as Florida's first openly autistic attorney, and I went viral on another continent in 2022 following the release of the Korean Netflix show *Extraordinary Attorney Woo* because there weren't many Korean autistic attorneys to speak with.

Despite a public presence, I don't like to make assumptions that people know most of the time, especially if it's someone I meet outside of my advocacy work or a disability-related space. Some people meet me through mutual acquaintances and don't know my whole life story. I also meet or speak with new people randomly, like when a person seated next to me on a long plane flight strikes up a conversation to pass the time. Chances are, these brand-new-to-me people have no idea I'm autistic unless I actually say something. I am not at liberty to guess if this is because of somebody's lack of knowledge and awareness of what diversity throughout the autism spectrum looks like or a commentary on my masking abilities.

Regardless of whether someone knows I am autistic, I don't know if they are cognizant of what my being autistic means—a lot of people might know that I am autistic as fact, but without the context or understanding of what exactly that means or how it affects *me*, let alone *them*. This is something that even my friends grapple with—they don't know how my disability affects them until I am overwhelmed in public or avoid trying something or give more details about a specific situation in my life, because, most of the time, "You're just Haley," as one of my best friends said when I asked. Simply, he continued, "Those are things that make you who you are." It did not take a deep, scientific explanation for my best friend to understand autism was why I was overwhelmed in a situation despite my intentions of explaining—he just shrugged it off and accepted I had had enough, and we moved on with our lives once I calmed down.

All of this is to say that having conversations where I have to tell people I am autistic can be rife with anxiety, involve careful planning, be spontaneous moments, be of little consequence, or lead to invasive lines of questioning. Disclosure is a form of mental gymnastics at times, but what really is it?

I'm glad you asked for more details! *Disclosure* refers to a variety of processes and tools that a person uses to share their disability status with others in order to receive *support*, *accommodations*, and *acceptance*. Autistics, disabled people, and their allies all have different roles to play in disclosure. While it appears to be something that falls squarely on autistic people at times, it also is a decision our family members, friends, employers, and others have to make as well, often for the same reasons. So, let's dive a little deeper into those key motivators of disclosure: support, accommodations, and acceptance.

Support

Sometimes, you just need someone in your life who "gets it." Support comes in many different shapes and sizes, depending on who you are. I'm sure what good support feels and looks like varies wildly from person to person, but to me, it's a level of somebody being a thoughtful listener while discussing a stressful day at work, a big hug when something great happens or after being startled during a scary movie, or someone you love holding your hand at a doctor's appointment.

When disclosing, support is a major motivator. In those situations, seeking and receiving support could look like:

- needing assistance, respite care, or someone to vent to as a caregiver
- advocating in order to receive disability benefits in adulthood
- receiving adequate medical care as a neurodivergent person
- making and finding friends within the autistic community.

Support more generally can also look like:

- advice
- information
- direction
- solutions
- competence
- guidance
- assistance.

These lists are far from exhaustive, but it's a start to figuring out what kind of support you might be hoping to give someone who shares with you about their disability (or the disability of someone they are close with—ideally, with that person's knowledge!).

Accommodations

This is the really big one for a lot of us, since accommodations are the one situation where disclosing a disability may be mandatory in order to receive support. *Accommodations* are changes that make something more accessible or doable for a person with a disability. Most formal accommodations happen at work or school, and do not make either of these things "easier." Basically, an accommodation at school doesn't mean a student with a disability will learn different or less difficult material, but it might allow them to better participate in the classroom or potentially involve a modification in how the curriculum is presented. They offer support for challenges without changing expectations for someone to do their job or learn.

In the United States, students with disabilities can receive accommodations under a few different federal laws: the Individuals with Disabilities in Education Act (IDEA), Section 504 of the Rehabilitation Act, or the Americans with Disabilities Act. For students in the K-12 system, typically IDEA or Section 504 will apply, while the Rehabilitation Act and the Americans with Disabilities Act are applicable in post-secondary programs. We will learn more about disability accommodations in school in a later chapter, but this is just a start to consider before we figure out how we can best advocate for ourselves as students and how other adults can advocate for us within the school environment.

Throughout the world, different laws dictate whether or not a person with a disability, including autism, can receive accommodations at work: in the U.S., this is Title I of the Americans with Disabilities Act; in the UK, this is the Equality Act; and in

Canada, this is the Accessible Canada Act. Typically, under any of these federal laws, a person has to have or share they have a disability in order to have protection from discrimination or access to accommodations that will help them face fewer barriers in employment.

Accommodations also don't always have to be super formal or just limited to work and school, but disclosing is a way to make sure we get those important modifications and changes made that allow us to be included in any place or activity that we would like to participate in. If others don't know what we need to join in, how would they know how to make something more accessible or take an individual's specific disability-related needs into account?

Acceptance

Of course, one of the main reasons neurodivergent people may disclose is to gain acceptance from their peers, supervisors, family members, partners, and others in life. It's hard having an aspect of who you are and unique traits that might make it difficult for others to understand you without context, or why you do the things you do. Most of the time I am sharing about my autism, and even certain things I am doing, I'm not always looking for an accommodation, but rather acceptance. If anything, autism helps *explain* my behavior and certain quirks of mine. Typically, the right people just nod along and innately "get it" and find these qualities and traits endearing and integral parts of who I am as a person.

Acceptance doesn't always have to come from neurotypical and nondisabled people, however. Sometimes, sharing with other people with autism or another disability is how we build community and find acceptance along with support from others.

And finally, there's one overarching theme in this: *self-acceptance*. It is difficult navigating this world as an autistic, neurodivergent, or otherwise disabled person. It is very easy to feel ashamed of the traits that make you different or embarrassed because your struggles look nothing like those of the folks around you. It can feel freeing and liberating to say aloud, not just to yourself, that you are autistic or neurodivergent—that something isn't "wrong" with you. That this is a part of who you are. Being more comfortable in your own skin and having that self-acceptance and confidence boost can make it more natural to be yourself and allow others around you to accept you for who you are, too.

Figuring out the goals

When I think about disclosure, I try to figure out what the goals usually are within that realm of support, accommodations, or acceptance. To best come up with ideas of what to expect and how to react depending on the situation, I think about which of those three things the person appears to be seeking—support, accommodations, or acceptance.

To me, support is the most complex goal that I can have when disclosing or when I'm the one being disclosed to. Sometimes, I share my autism-related struggles because I want to vent or have an empathetic friend listen to me. Sometimes, I do want advice for handling a sensory or social situation, or the advice comes unsolicited. Allies who disclose may have entirely different goals than I do, such as the parents who need respite, a referral to a specialist to help their child, or further advocacy at the child's school or with government services.

If they need accommodations, it's much more matter-of-fact and less emotional, but it can be incredibly nerve-wracking to ask to begin with. If I'm requesting accommodations, I tend to be a little bit more anxious than when I talk to my friends or other people in my life. That is because it concerns my rights as a person with a disability and requires a heck of a lot more self-advocacy skills to ensure clear communication, most often in a professional setting (more on workplace accommodations later!).

Usually, if that person wants acceptance, they want a kind, nonjudgmental friend or listener who is empathetic in attempting to understand and validate them. I find these situations the most intuitive to navigate, since oftentimes it's another autistic or neurodivergent person who trusts me and feels safe sharing and wants to find or build a community of people who simply "get it," although that isn't always the case.

Once I know the goals, it makes what I plan to say or how I react a lot easier. When I speak, I can determine how much information to share. For example, if someone invited me out to an overwhelming place for an event or to go out with friends, I might say, "That sounds fun! But I'm autistic and it's really difficult for me to be in a loud and crowded place. Can we maybe go somewhere quieter?" As a reactor, I know whether I am expected to be a good listener, provide thoughtful advice, keep quiet, or connect somebody to solutions, strategies, or potential allies and friends.

CHAPTER 3

DISCLOSING FOR PARENTS
Talking to Neurodivergent Kids About Themselves

M Y PARENTS QUITE LIKELY TOLD ME about my autism in the best way possible. I was nine years old, and it was the summer before starting the fourth grade. Most Florida summers when I grew up were similar—lots of fun days by the pool, arts and crafts, drawing, reading books, and playing video games in my spare time. Sometimes, my mom and I would even read books together by the pool. One book series at this time that particularly captivated my heart was the Harry Potter series. It was 2003, and the Harry Potter phenomenon was sweeping the world following the release of the first two movies (*Harry Potter and the Sorcerer's Stone* and *Harry Potter and the Chamber of Secrets*) and a new fifth installment in the book series. Naturally, it became one of my most passionate autistic special interests. That year for my birthday, I had a Harry Potter-themed party (we even shared a prophetic July 31 birthday!), I collected Harry Potter figurines and collectibles, and I built all of the Harry Potter Lego sets…you get the idea. There was no doubt that young Haley was enamored, perhaps obsessed, with the Harry Potter universe.

For my family, the intense interest in Harry Potter was exactly what they needed to tell me about my autism. It was a surefire way to get me interested in having a serious conversation about myself. My parents began by simply saying, "You have magical powers just like Harry Potter," and, of course, being so young, I was going to believe this and want to hear more. My initial reaction to that strong start was that I, too, was a witch or wizard, and so were my parents—when I would turn 11, an owl would arrive through a window delivering my acceptance letter to Hogwarts School of Witchcraft and Wizardry, and then I would find my true path and be able to do all sorts of cool magic stuff.

My hopes of being a wizard just like Harry were quickly dashed when the magic in me was quickly transformed into autism. This was not a bad thing, however. Like Harry, I had magic in me—I was creative, sensitive, passionate, a good listener, mature for my age, smart with a photographic memory. I was also different because of my autism. Harry Potter was different, too. He grew up in the home of non-magical relatives and was labeled weird, a freak, and excluded among them. He was also treated differently among the witches and wizards because he was the famous Boy Who Lived and had a lightning bolt scar across his forehead as a constant reminder of his differences.

I had some, albeit not much, familiarity with autism before this conversation. As I mentioned in Chapter 1, my only frame of reference was a book from *The Baby-Sitters Club* series called *Kristy and the Secret of Susan*. To recap: Susan was largely nonspeaking, but had a photographic memory for dates and songs and went to a segregated "special" school, and the babysitter wanted to keep her included within the community. I didn't feel like I had a lot in common with Susan because I was in a mainstream school, was not musically inclined, and, of course, was speaking. With this knowledge in mind, my parents were able to color in the full picture of the spectrum and how there are varying abilities, strengths, and weaknesses that people with autism might have. Some people, like Susan, had intellectual disabilities and savant-like skills, while others, like me, did not.

To make the most of this day (and the coming summer days) and to ensure I understood myself and autism, my mom later pulled out a workbook, which we went through together, filling out the parts that felt important and relevant; the most recent edition of the one we used is Catherine Flaherty's *Autism: What Does it Mean to Me?* (2014). I remember thinking I had magic in me, after all, and left these seemingly deep talks with a sense of pride and feeling as though I had a better understanding of the things that made me who I am.

The workbook was one of many books and resources my parents collected over the years. Eventually, my mother would introduce me to the work of other autistic women in particular—specifically, Temple Grandin and Liane Holliday Willey. Jennifer Cook is another strong, female autistic voice worth turning to for further insight. I later discovered my mom had a large library of autism books in her closet, readying herself and my dad for all aspects of my development, and to eventually aid me in my own understanding as well. The omissions from this book collection are things that uniquely inspired me as an autistic writer—books by and for autistic people about middle school, the college/university years, for lawyers where our existence as autistics was largely ignored except for a few books about interacting with the legal system as an accused person or perpetrator, and for those of us figuring out how to be independent adults. Other books were absolute delights whose authors eventually became friends and colleagues, and there are so many more resources out there today that parents and caregivers alike can use as valuable teaching tools and which I'm sure my family would have been eager to have, and younger me would've delighted in reading and checking out.

What initially shaped and molded my worldview on autism was my parents' repurposing of the Harry Potter series—more so than the many resources and lack thereof that would eventually influence my career path and advocacy journey. I look back on that lazy summer afternoon as the years go by. The discovery of autism through the lens of a series I loved taught me self-love, nurtured my special interests and passions, and instilled confidence in me while living in a world rife with ableism and other biases, where autistic people are either overtly or subtly told, "Be yourself, but not like that." Instead, my parents set me up to be proud of who I am and defy the expectations of how I "should" feel about having a disability.

This continued as I got older. Sure, my interest in Harry Potter waned as I became a teenager and other passions and hobbies took a front seat in my life, but the life lessons stayed the same. Like many teenagers, my self-confidence would waver. I wondered for the first time what it might be like to be neurotypical, to not have to struggle socially, to be popular and make friends as everyone else around me seemingly did without much effort. Having gone to three schools in three years and not finding "my people," I really wanted these answers, thinking being some kind of "normal" would be a magic bullet to my problems (it was not). Instead, I felt isolated, confused, and stressed. But one of those big conversations about autism happened, not with my family, but with a family friend who aptly described me as being "perfect in an imperfect world." Essentially, I was designed to be exactly who I am, and that is a form of perfection; sure, we're all flawed human beings and that's part of being alive, but the world is the truly wrong, flawed place for not recognizing the perfect imperfections of everybody's humanity and instead wanting more conformity. It was exactly the message that I needed at the time.

The conversations also became deeper as I became more involved in private and public advocacy. We would talk about if I would tell my friends or guys I would date, and how. We would strategize which of my friends' parents we wanted to know so they could better accommodate me in activities and gatherings. Knowing about my autism meant I was more of an active participant in meetings with teachers and other professionals at school. It meant that when the opportunity arose to speak at an autism conference and tell my story, I seized it. When I was writing my first book, one of the big conversations we had was whether or not I wanted to use my real name or a pen name for my book. I decided on my own name because I felt comfortable enough with my own story at the time, not thinking much about how that would stretch into my future and eventually shape my adult life.

The conversations we have now have morphed yet again now that I am fully independent and have evolved as I learn more about myself and my community. I have language for experiences and ideas I never had before; now I can tell you when and what overwhelms me, and that I am out of sorts from it, or that maybe I feel the way I do because I haven't eaten all day and my stomach never sent the hunger cues. I can articulate the many things that make being autistic what it is, and in turn, it allows me to be the teacher rather than the student nowadays. Finally, it feels like I have so many answers my younger self did not. Autism explains why certain experiences are overwhelming for me, but now I can explain what parts of those experiences are overwhelming and difficult—for example, when I hear jazz music and it makes me feel seriously anxious and dysregulated, I can now tell you it's the sound of the saxophone that sends my ears and senses into overdrive and high alert that leaves me feeling exhausted and flighty.

How to tell your child

Parents regularly ask me how my parents talked to me about autism that very first time, and why they decided it was the "right" time. I decided to ask them about it. My mom and dad felt there was never really going to be a "right" time, but they decided I was mature enough and at a point in my life when it made sense to at least introduce autism to me. I was old enough to do some things by myself, but young enough to need more supervision and guidance from others.

I also asked my parents about how they seemed to embrace neurodiversity at the time (they admit they had not been familiar with the word in the early 2000s), really leaning into that I was different and focusing on my strengths instead of my weaknesses. My dad explained that kids (and adults) usually know when things are hard for them, or what they aren't good at. Even as adults, and if you've ever been in a supervisory position at work or an employee before, you know what people are not good at or where they are underperforming since they often receive criticism about those traits or actions. It is less often somebody knows they are doing a good job, he said, reminding me I should continue to acknowledge when people do something well and not just when they need more support or are falling short somewhere. The same, he and my mom decided, goes for kids. Chances are, according to my mom, I was already pretty aware of what was hard for me: playing sports, making friends, sharing my emotions, loud and crowded places, certain motor skills that were autism related and not left-handed related, note-taking, organizing, and keeping my room clean. I knew this stuff was hard for me, and I am aware at this point in my life those things are still hard for me!

Don't hide the truth

When I was a psychology major in college, I took a class on developmental psychology to understand how children progressed, grew, and learned. While I don't remember many of the specifics beyond Piaget's theory of cognitive development and its four stages, one thing did stand out for me at the end of the course: *children are far more perceptive and intelligent than adults give them credit for.*

It's no secret that with a disability, many things are harder for your child. There is a very good chance they are aware of this! Even as a little kid, I knew there were things other kids did fairly easily, like tying their shoelaces, which I struggled greatly with (it took me a while to figure that one out). I also knew I spent more time with adults than my peers did, but initially brushed this off due to being an only child and not having any similar-aged cousins. I was used to adults playing with me and my varied toys and games because there weren't many other kids around me outside of school, and I was too shy, clumsy, and not very outdoorsy to go out and play with the neighborhood kids who didn't go to my school. Adults were always more of "my people" who happily participated in my world of pretend, action figures, Legos, Playmobil, and other toys, and maybe actually didn't lose on purpose and let me· win at board games.

I didn't distinguish any differences when I was being shuttled to speech or occupational therapy sessions after school, or even when I was younger and they would come to the house. These were yet more adults who would play with me, often using strategies and toys and games to teach me social, conversational, and motor skills. Other times, there would be an autism-related professional observing me or my classroom to give input for greater inclusion and accessibility, but I must have thought they were there for everybody and not just me.

However, because of this unique worldview that truly revolved around adults more than children my own age, I did miss one key thing that a lot of neurodivergent kids pick up on pretty early on: they are somehow "different" from their peers. *Your child probably knows they are different.* Looking back, this should have been obvious to me: I was not like the other girls. All of my friends were boys. I was the only girl on the playground who traded Pokémon and Yu-Gi-Oh cards and would play video games in my free time when I was done with my homework. I was always picked last in gym class to join the team due to what was probably the perfect combination of clumsiness and social awkwardness. I had a phase where I was really into Ancient Egypt. I was reading more advanced chapter books than the rest of the class, seemingly always had the answers to the teacher's questions, and even would get more difficult math homework at one point to keep me academically challenged. I was also a frequent visitor to the nurse's office with stomach aches that, looking back, I am confident were likely more the result of nervousness or needing quiet than actual food disagreeing with my insides. Putting all of these things together, I was probably a "weird" kid, but a delightfully happy one at that.

The main reason I didn't know I was different is because my parents were also experts at distraction. I knew I was socially excluded and didn't fit in, but they had me convinced I was the coolest person on the planet. I remember being about seven years old and being the only kid in my classroom who was not invited to a classmate's birthday party. Instead of dwelling on this and continually advocating for my inclusion as they often did (though in this situation, to no avail), my parents took me out for ice cream and a visit to the toy store on the day of the party. I pretty much forgot somebody even had a birthday party that weekend because my ice-cream-and-toy-store outing was far more exciting.

Neurodivergent kids know when they are different and already have nagging suspicions that something separates them from their neurotypical friends and classmates. They know when they are being taken out of activities to receive services. From a young age, neurodivergent kids begin struggling with self-esteem. Kids with learning disabilities are often told they are lazy or stupid and should try harder (Greenfest, 2016). Having an honest conversation with a neurodivergent young person about a brain-based condition that makes it harder for them to learn, read, do math, socialize with others, or manage their emotions can help boost confidence and self-esteem without making them feel ashamed of these school-related challenges that their peers may wrongly give them a hard time about.

In particular, autistic youth are more likely to be bullied than our neurotypical counterparts, so we already know what it's like to be treated differently in a negative way from our peers. In fact, over 60 percent of autistic youth in the United States and around 61 percent of children and teenagers with autism in the United Kingdom are bullied (Autism Speaks, 2024; Connolly, 2014). This is especially true in the teenage years, where social differences become more apparent with peer interactions and relationships becoming more complex and nuanced. With autistic youth experiencing high rates of bullying and harassment at the hands of their peers, their disability-related traits may be more apparent and lead to further questions of *why* they are being treated and perceived so negatively. While that is obviously a problem on the bully's side—a lack of tolerance, problems at home, prejudice, you name it—it doesn't change the impact that these moments of cruelty have on autistic young people, whose mental health, self-esteem, confidence, and identity can all be affected. Knowing you are different from your peers because of bullying and social exclusion raises a lot of questions, and finding answers is also very possible beyond adults denying and deflecting. Even being in segregated classrooms, or receiving accommodations or special education services, is merely enough to attract attention from neurotypical students and also cause autistic students to notice differences in their schedules, academic course offerings, classmates, and friendship-making potential.

Peers of mine who were young adults discovered autism as a possible explanation for traits and behavior through spending time with other autistic people, university course-work, or even posts and videos on TikTok, Instagram, Tumblr, and Facebook that raised a question of "I might be autistic" and required further research. Even if a *why* is being withheld or is currently unknown for one of many reasons that lead to people being undiagnosed, as I noted earlier, kids are smarter than we give them credit for and are fully capable of finding out about autism by themselves.

On the flip side, "hiding the truth," hoping that your autistic children won't know they are autistic, can have severe consequences in your parent–child relationship, and possibly in your child's future. My mom has told me countless stories of parents she met along our journey who would deny their kid's diagnosis, or who would refuse to have them evaluated when there was suspicion that the kid might be autistic for fear of labeling them. This type of shame was unique in its denial. "When you deny, you deny your child," she would say. This denial of diagnosis out of fear meant many children and teenagers we knew were denied chances at evaluation, special education services, speech and occupational therapy that could prove helpful, receiving accommodations, tailored plans to help them learn social and conversational skills, and more.

Many people who were denied a diagnosis develop incredible masking skills that lead to burnout and other mental health issues from a lifetime of learning the dominant social language from television, books, and movies, and observing and mimicking others' behavior. They may later discover they are autistic through social media, licensed professionals, or recommendations from peers or friends, and this discovery is life-changing, either positively or negatively. When these late-discovered autistics eventually confront their families who "always thought that might be the case" or somehow were in denial along the way, it may create a rift in the relationship due to the lack of trust or the parents' ableism and shame around the stigma of an autism diagnosis, and the child's realization that they could have—should have—had support much earlier if only their caregivers had sought out a diagnosis and used the knowledge to improve quality of life in educational settings, relationships, and more.

My heart breaks for those autistic people navigating the world who don't know they are autistic and never find this information, who spent a lifetime as autistic people not knowing who they were or why they may have been different and struggled along the way, without ever receiving proper support. While they may or may not be okay without this knowledge, the idea that it was potentially taken from them early on due to somebody else's fear of autism is its own kind of sad.

The flip side of "hiding the truth" is something I discovered through a former friend of mine a few years ago—when the family knows a child is autistic, but chooses to withhold that information for too long or until the child confronts them. This person told me about an autism diagnosis earlier in life. He had explained to me that his family considered him "cured" since he was now an adult with a successful career, was college-educated, and lived independently. However, he regularly socially alienated others and was unaware of the impact of his words and actions, with others often mistaking him for being rude and aloof. He eventually shared with me that his parents only told him he was autistic once he reached adulthood so he could be more aware of his own medical history. I asked what he knew about autism; truthfully, he knew very little, instead denying he would be saying or doing things others considered inappropriate that were in fact related to his disability. If I asked any questions in an attempt to be more supportive, they were summarily dismissed with obvious discomfort around the topic. I realized he was never given the tools to advocate for his disability-related needs or had much of an opportunity to form a positive disability identity. I realized his shame around autism stemmed from the family.

Another scenario is when the family never says anything, due to that same shame and stigma my friend felt and his family experienced. When I was writing and researching an article for *Well + Good* about how a lot of autistic women, nonbinary people, and transgender people go undiagnosed or late diagnosed, I spoke with a transgender woman who discovered she was autistic when she was well into adulthood after a slew of visits with professionals, psychological incidents, and prescription medications. For her, an autism diagnosis was a lightbulb moment, and her self-discovery has since brought a lot of joy and pride. However, when she spoke to her parents about her new autism identification, they told her she had been diagnosed with autism as a child, leading her to learn she had spent years masking, enduring confusion and bullying. Her parents chose not to tell her or pursue services to help due to the stigma of autism while she was growing up; she credited this decision with the masking, bullying, emotional pain, and confusion (Moss, 2022). This story harkened back to my mom's adage of "when you deny, you deny your child"—leaving me wondering about the autistic kids whose families knew and declined services and support due to the stigma within their communities.

Stigma and shame are real, and research suggests they exist in schools, workplaces, families, communities, and pretty much everywhere (Turnock, Langley, & Jones, 2022). There are different factors that influence stigma, including cultural differences. But one of the first steps to reducing the stigma around autism, neurodiversity, and disability is confronting it head-on at home before working to dismantle it everywhere else in the world.

Use developmentally appropriate language

Disability rights advocate Marie Dagenais-Lewis said something in a *HuffPost* article about talking to kids about disability that really stuck with me: "Parents of the next generations hold a key when it comes to dismantling the ableist society by teaching the next generations to embrace disability as diversity" (Bologna, 2021). This seems like a lot, but what she is saying is that parents are ultimately responsible for teaching their kids—disabled, nondisabled, neurotypical, and neuro-divergent—how to talk about disability and get used to the idea that everyone's brains and bodies act in unique ways. It doesn't mean we all have to have an education background or study disability at the university level like I did for my minor in college, nor does it mean we have to expect youngsters to have an advanced understanding of ableism, disability rights, or accessibility.

I am often asked if there is a "right age" to have these types of conversations, and the more I think about it, the more I'm inclined to say no. There is no perfect age or age-appropriate time to talk to a kid about their autism or disability as a whole. Assuming someone's age matches their likely level of under-standing is outdated and underestimates their potential to learn. Each child develops on their own timeline, with some having higher levels of understanding earlier than others, or more emotional maturity down the line.

Sometimes, *the simplest explanations are the best ones.* It's really easy to get so bogged down in language, disability culture, and our own education that we forget we're dealing with young people who will need some modeling and wording to make sense of the world around them. Your explanations can be as simple as "Your brain works differently than somebody else's. Do you know how you find this really calming? Other people might find this scary!" You can tie this back to their interests and things that feel natural that any little one can understand.

You don't need to be a neurodiversity expert or have the "right" language

Here's the thing—a lot of us are nervous about having these talks with our children because we want them to have a positive experience, but also we don't know if we're going to get it right ourselves. The autism discourse has changed greatly since I was first diagnosed, with discussions about neurodiversity entering the mainstream. When I was diagnosed in the late 1990s, my parents certainly had never heard of neurodiversity, a term that did not come into existence until 1998, and the modern self-advocacy movement wasn't fully shaped or known in parent circles the way it is today due to popularity of the internet and social media. With a lot of new vocabulary and social nuance, getting an identity discussion right (especially if it is not one you share with your child) can feel tricky and intimidating.

However, you don't have to have the perfect language of neurodiversity to be a great ally as a parent or caregiver. My parents probably did not know the term *neurodiversity* existed until I was in college, probably around 2014-ish, by which time I had come across it and learned more. By then, the first Harry Potter discussion was well in the rearview mirror of my life. Yet, despite not having the vocabulary, that initial "different is neither better nor worse—it's just different, and different can be extraordinary" discussion was exactly what neurodiversity is about: we all have different brains! Don't let modern terminology get in the way of your instincts to be the best advocate, ally, and trusted adult you could be in your child's life; instead, language is just another tool to celebrate and help people be understood.

If you do feel you need a crash course on disability-related language, here are some things I'd keep in mind. I tried to put these in plain language so anybody can understand, regardless of age or ability:

- *Neurodiversity.* This is the idea that we all have different brains. No one brain is better or worse. We all think differently, and no two people experience the world in the exact same way.

- *Neurotypical.* This is how the majority of brains work based on what society and others expect of you. You do not find most things overwhelming and naturally understand the "rules" based on culture and socializing. Note: this is not the same as "normal." Whenever I talk to children (and adults!), I ask them what "normal" is, and they rarely have a good answer other than a setting on the washing machine.

- *Neurodivergent.* This is when a person's brain works and thinks outside of what is expected. If a person is not neurotypical, they are neurodivergent. ADHD, autism, developmental disabilities, intellectual disabilities, learning disabilities, and mental health disabilities are all types of neurodivergence (Moss, 2021).

Person-first vs. identity-first language

A lot of people get really hung up on the idea of whether or not they are going to be using person-first language or identity-first language before even getting started on any disability conversation! The history and understanding of both linguistic choices and movements are complex, and vary greatly from person to person. *Person-first language* came about as a way to be respectful, to remember to put the person before a disability to fight dehumanization efforts and fight stigma, signaling that a disability does not make someone less of a person. Examples of this would be saying "Haley has autism," "Haley is a person with a disability," or "Haley is a woman with autism."

Identity-first language is preferred among the autistic community, because being autistic is regarded as a facet of a person's identity, rather than a source of shame (Ladau, 2015).

Here is a quick summary or easy ways to explain this if you ever feel like it comes up or you don't really know or want to get into the details:

- *Autistic (identity-first language).* Some people view autism as part of who they are and choose to use "autistic" to describe themselves, just like I may describe myself as a redhead. *Neurodivergent* also is considered a form of identity-first-language.

- *Has autism (person-first language).* Some people want to separate autism from themselves and look at it as something else and don't see it as integral to who they are, just like I may say I have red hair.

We all describe ourselves in certain ways depending on the situation and how we feel about ourselves, and that's totally okay! I use "autistic" for myself because I don't think I am "with autism"—it's not something I can set down and forget about, like where I put my keys when I got home last night and then I am "without my keys." However, I honestly won't get upset or correct you if you say I have autism; I'm just glad you're engaging and trying to have conversations that some people shy away from entirely because they're so hung up on the language and "getting it right" that they don't even bother trying. If you really don't know what to say, just admit it—it's okay to ask!

Even then, keep in mind a few key things:

- It's okay not to have disability language or to understand the history or the *why* behind certain word choices when talking about autism.

- Be respectful of how somebody describes themselves— chances are, it's a personal decision and can mean a lot to them or be a big part of their individual journey.

- You can still be affirming and understanding without

ever using vocabulary related to neurodiversity. Some of the greatest allies and neurotypical advocates I know lack a theoretical or communal understanding of the disabled experience, but they are in sync with what is going on and are naturally super accepting and strive for what feels right in a human way, which makes these interactions as positive as possible, especially with young people.

Answering questions from your child

We already talked about how hiding the truth can lead to a later self-discovery, resentment, or a potential conflict between you and your child, but kids are naturally curious as well. Sometimes they're going to have questions even after you tell them about their autism, neurodivergence, or disability. They might even have questions you don't have answers to—and that's okay!

Whenever you are answering questions, it's important to do so honestly and accurately with the best, truthful information you have access to. While I am not a parent, I have highlighted some common questions that youngsters have asked me over the years and how I'd answer them today now that I've had some time to think about them.

One curious question that children will ask me is *whether they were born with autism or if they got it from somebody else* (the adult's version of this question will likely come in the form of a vaccine junk science question). An autistic kid might be worried they did something wrong or be curious if you feel any type of "guilt." You might want to answer that doctors and scientists right now think people are born with autism, but the experts and family members, like you, don't always know right away. Science might learn more, but for now, that's the best answer we've got. If a child asks how long you've known, just be honest, and make sure to reassure them that you love them for who they are! Another version of this question is how someone "gets" autism, and I explain you can't catch it like a cold—again, explaining people are born that way, just like some of us are born with different eye and hair colors or extra or missing fingers and toes, for instance—it just is that way. It's nobody's "fault" and you can't spread or catch autism.

Usually, since I talk about my special interests and passions with kids, *the most common question they have for me is about my favorite Pokémon.* I purposely talk about Pokémon with them since out of all of the interests and games I've played throughout my life, it's one of the few franchises still going strong, and many of them can relate to interacting with through trading cards, the TV series, or video games. It isn't so much an autism question as a human connection question. It's my favorite "autism" question since they are merely viewing me as an adult who understands their favorite games or animated series. If anything, it means children think I am cool, which is not an experience I am used to having, so I enjoy it. By the way, if you're now wondering too, my all-time favorite Pokémon is Vulpix, and I always pick the fire-type starters in the games.

A few things I think make questions and conversations easier

One common thread I've felt and I know other autistic people have shared is some form of isolation or loneliness, as if you are the only person in the world going through this. For several years, I never knew any autistic people outside of the few autistic adult experts and authors my parents had exposed me to through their written work. I didn't know about the everyday autistic people I would find community with, or the many friends I would make along the way. It turns out that most of the time I meet other neurodivergent people today, there is sort of an innate mutual understanding, or, as some have described it, "a vibe" that you pick up on and immediately strike up a kinship. Thanks to those relationships and additional knowledge, I no longer feel so alone and have some ideas to make you feel more empowered.

Having access to great books that are appropriate for any age and stage

Personally, I love to read. I collect autism-, neurodiversity-, and disability-related books of all kinds to assist people of all ages in their understanding and point them to resources. I read fiction, nonfiction, memoirs and biographies, and deep dives. Sure, I have read Steve Silberman's *NeuroTribes*, Eric Garcia's *We're Not Broken*, Dr. Devon Price's *Unmasking Autism*, and Barry Prizant's *Uniquely Human* cover to cover, and enjoyed all of them, but these are reads I used for my own education and wouldn't necessarily use with younger children; teenagers, maybe, if they want to go in-depth and appreciate the density, history, and rich storytelling these nonfiction touchstones of autism books have to offer. I've recommended them to my university students when I taught classes in the psychology department. But I wouldn't use them to sit down with a preteen or elementary school-aged kid and expect them to stay engaged for very long—unless, of course, they really wanted to or also loved to read adult nonfiction.

Some of the best things I've used as teaching tools for kids, teenagers, and adults alike are picture books. Some of them have been awesome conversation starters. When I was in my first lawyer job, I had a copy of *All Cats Have Asperger Syndrome* (which is now *All Cats Are on the Autism Spectrum*) on my desk. It made my clients and colleagues (mostly all adults) feel comfortable asking me about and learning about autism, and we had a good laugh out of some of the funny cat pictures. The best part was my mom first bought the book for me when I was 13 and thought I was too old and too cool for picture books. I couldn't have been more wrong—I had a feeling of pure joy and even more acceptance upon reading the book, and I actually used it to teach my friends in high school as well. *All Cats* was such an impactful and positive tool in my disclosure and personal acceptance toolbox that the author, Kathy Hoopmann, asked me to write the foreword for the updated edition a few years back.

One thing I particularly love about today's literary landscape is the availability of *#OwnVoices stories* about neurodiversity—these are books about neurodivergent characters and people, written by neurodivergent authors, so we're moving past the days of my confusion with *The Baby-Sitters Club* (the author was a former special education teacher actually), and having fictional stories about autistic characters written by real autistic people, when the autism isn't always central to the plot. When I interviewed autistic authors for the We Need Diverse Books blog, one autistic author, Jen Malia, explained to me how one of her books about a seven-year-old who loves science and was nervous about the sensory experience of a new science experiment wasn't a story about autism as much as it was a story about a girl who happened to be autistic. Usually, when other people tell our stories, it's autism stories where we aren't the main characters or they feel too prescriptive in what we're supposed to look and act like. I wrote then, "No autistic young reader should feel alone or that they don't identify with how neurotypicals view them; they deserve access to stories of acceptance and empowerment" (Moss, 2020), and I still believe that to be the case to make so many conversations that they will have throughout their lives so much easier.

If you aren't sure where to turn to find updates and more recommendations and thoughts about neurodiversity in children's literature, the blog A Novel Mind by autistic author Sally J. Pla is a phenomenal place to read reviews, ideas, and author interviews and profiles on their inspiration behind their work (www.anovelmind.com).

Here are some of my all-time favorite autism books that help normalize and explain autism in a friendly way to children in particular, and which may guide you in sharing information and gaining practical strategies to use with autistic youth. Many are authored by autistics. I'm also giving a recap of some of the ones mentioned and why they may be helpful resources:

- *Ask and Tell: Self-Advocacy and Disclosure for People on the Autism Spectrum* edited by Stephen M. Shore (for all ages, but great for parents and self-advocates), which actually inspired the premise of this book. It's two decades old now and a lot has changed, but it really focuses on self-advocates while I hope to help everybody out along the way.

- *My Brother Otto* by Meg Raby (picture book) is written from a sibling's perspective about having a nonspeaking autistic brother.

- *Come Meet Drayden* by Dana Young-Askew (picture book), again written from a sibling perspective, shows how much representation truly matters for families.

- *A Day with No Words* by Tiffany Hammond is a gorgeous book by an autistic mother of autistic sons about how communication comes in many forms and can transcend spoken language.

- *All Cats Are on the Autism Spectrum* (picture book for all ages) is just one of my favorite books to ever exist—at the very least, you can delight in the cute cat pictures.

- *Different Like Me: My Book of Autism Heroes* by Jennifer Elder (picture book) is a great way to introduce children to people throughout history who were likely autistic. It's a great introduction to encourage a sense of pride and to ease feelings of being the only one on the spectrum.

- *Wired Differently: 30 Neurodivergent People You Should*

Know by Joe Wells is similar but it includes more forms of neurodiversity such as ADHD and learning disabilities in addition to autism.

Of course, this isn't exhaustive, but these are some of the books I've recommended to teachers for their classrooms, libraries for their young readers, and, of course, family members like you for your children, young relatives, siblings, and more.

Having friends with disabilities or knowing other people in the community

At this point in my life, I am lucky to have the opportunity to make a lot of new acquaintances and friends. Some of my favorite new friends are neurotypical parents of autistic children. One of my friends has a young daughter with autism as well as a neurotypical son. Her daughter is not the only reason we are friends—we talk about everything, from school horror stories to run-of-the-mill gossip and shared interests. But some of our best conversations are where she vulnerably turns to me for parenting advice. A few days ago, she came to me explaining both of her children were invited to a birthday party at a kids' restaurant that specializes in being loud, bright, and high-energy. It sounds like a sensory onslaught. She had texted me to say that both of her children were invited to this two-hour birthday party, but she had only intended to bring her son, thinking it would be too much for her autistic daughter to handle because of the loud, contained environment compared to more kinetic sensory-seeking experiences like jumping on a trampoline or even a theme park—but my friend was questioning if her daughter would enjoy the party or be too overwhelmed. The neighborhood kid and her daughter loved hanging out together. I asked if her daughter wanted to go in the first place due to the friendship between the kids. Then I wondered, if perhaps the restaurant became too much to handle, whether there was an exit strategy that might not impact everybody's ability to have a good time. My perspective was that social exclusion as an autistic person is tough and shouldn't inadvertently begin at home, and maybe it's best not to miss opportunities even if it's well intended (this circles back to benevolent ableism).

It turns out having an autistic friend to help advocate and come up with solutions is a good thing—my friend's daughter stayed for 90 minutes, where she went bowling, saw the birthday kid, ate some pizza, and even hugged the restaurant mascot before saying she wanted to go home. Without that extra advocacy push or perspective from me, which helped her mom rethink her plan for the day, I don't know if this youngster would've had the opportunity to be included. It's these moments that grow a friendship. It made me realize how much neurotypical parents need to put themselves in their child's shoes, and one way to help do that is knowing autistic adults who have walked in similar shoes before.

I know one day, when my friend feels ready to talk to her daughter about autism, it will be infinitely less isolating than it is for many of us, because my friend can say, "You know our friend Haley? She is autistic, like you," and her daughter will immediately have someone who isn't a stranger or public figure to relate to.

Sometimes, the advice I give to curious parents is to go make friends with autistic and neurodivergent adults within your community. You can do this through online groups, connecting with local nonprofit organizations, or even tapping into your network of existing friends—chances are, you already do have at least one autistic and/or neurodivergent friend and just never really gave it much thought. (True story: over the years, I found out almost all my friends are neurodivergent because that is who I naturally gravitated towards, and who naturally gravitated towards me. I often knew they were before they did.)

First off, autistic people make awesome friends. We are loyal, kind, and thoughtful, with a good sense of humor. If we share similar hobbies, we will absolutely nerd out with you. Second, if we feel comfortable with you and you learn to communicate with us in a way that feels safe and doesn't put all the pressure on us to mask, you'll get a window into perhaps how your children may be experiencing the world. Don't be too quick to assume it is the exact same perception—just maybe an explanation or viewpoint you haven't considered. It'll make you a stronger advocate, and I promise your local autistic adult will be happy to have a genuine friend (of course, if you are genuine and not just using them for parenting advice) since making friends is difficult and frustrating, especially as an adult. Plus, if your children know us, we might be able to impart our wisdom and befriend them, too—and one day, explaining that bond and common diagnosis to them can be life-changing as well. Besides, having role models you can call friends is just exciting. I certainly respect and enjoy my parent friends, and hope they feel the same way about me.

Knowing at least one or two "famous" people or characters with similar characteristics or who are also autistic

If you need some inspiration for "famous" people, two of my favorite books that I highlighted earlier make this real. They are *Different Like Me: My Book of Autism Heroes* and *Wired Differently: 30 Neurodivergent People You Should Know*. These two books cover the gamut of famous figures throughout history from Sir Isaac Newton all the way to modern icons like Olympic gymnast and gold medalist Simone Biles (again, I really love books, but if you don't like to read, knowing people like Newton and Biles are neurodivergent is great to aid in your explanations to give your young people some new role models that they may be familiar with already and have something in common with). Putting together a list of celebrities, innovators, and historical figures that your child may relate to can help ease the confusion or shock of a diagnosis being shared with them. Bonus points if the people you find and use as examples share similar passions or contribute to some kind of occupation or interest your child wants to be part of when they grow up.

If you need some contemporary examples of real-life autistic people (every time I ask people to name a famous autistic person, at least one person is completely at a loss), you can always find resources such as articles, books, and videos about public figures like Greta Thunberg, Elon Musk, and Temple Grandin. There is something cool about saying you have something in common with people who have advocated for climate change reform, built new technologies, and revolutionized animal care. How is that not a self-esteem boost to make someone feel less alone?

Fiction also is a great place to turn if the real-life autistic and neurodivergent people aren't doing the trick for your discussions. You'd be surprised how much mileage I have gotten out of conversations that jumpstarted out of familiar fictional characters, like Julia on *Sesame Street*. It's very easy to naturally show or watch someone like Julia and explain, "You know how Julia might not look at Big Bird? That's because, like you, she finds it hard, but she's listening to everything he says." If you need some other examples of autistic or likely-to-be-autistic/relatable characters in particular (I'm not opining on whether or not they are "accurate," since you know what might work best for you or your family), you might find your young person relates heavily to Hermione in *Harry Potter* (I certainly did, as a girl who always raised her hand and knew all the answers), Lilo from *Lilo & Stitch*, Twyla from *Monster High*, Sheldon from *The Big Bang Theory*, or even whole shows that revolve around autism like *Atypical* and *The Good Doctor*. While some autistic representations on television and in the movies may feel stereotypical or like a collection of checklist traits, they are often a great jumping-off point for conversation, especially if the autistic young person you know relates to them—which is all that matters. Feeling seen and represented is important and contributes to the "you are not alone" message you'll hopefully want to instill in them. With so few relatable characters out there for us that don't make us feel like aliens or curious oddities, representation matters.

CHAPTER 4

DISCLOSING FOR PARENTS
Trusting and Telling Other Kids and Adults

E VEN IF YOU HAVEN'T TALKED TO YOUR CHILD about their autism, strengths, and weaknesses, that doesn't mean it's an off-limits conversation with other family members and people you and your family will encounter. Siblings are aware of their autistic sibling's differences and challenges, how each person in the household is being treated, and how time is spent and resources are shared. Other family members might be part of your household, or check in regularly, or be a huge part of your child's life. How we approach these dynamics is sensitive and unique.

And, of course, there are non-familial situations—friends who feel like family, as well as total strangers in public, the community, or even on the internet. There's no one-size-fits-all answer to talking about autism and related conditions with all of these people, but we can do our best to decide when and what is appropriate to share, especially if our young people are unable to do it themselves.

Talking to siblings and other family members

Ah, families. You love them. You have members of your family
you despise or who annoy you, and others who are your rock
and make you feel loved, safe, and supported. You have the
relatives you see and catch up with several times a year on
major holidays and birthdays, and ones you talk to all the
time. Others live with you or your autistic loved one, and
are very aware of the differences that autism makes to your
life. A diagnosis can bring feelings of clarity, anger, grief, or
relief—and having trusted relatives by your side can make a
positive impact in your life and also lead to questions, opportunities for advocacy, and the need to have some necessary
conversations with those around you. We're going to unpack
all of the major family relations together and how to navigate
the many questions, situations, and feelings that come along
with them.

Aunts, uncles, grandparents, cousins, and other relatives—oh my!

I come from a small family, and it's very easy as a caregiver
to feel isolated, as my parents have told me. They were faced
with skepticism and denial from our community and sometimes even family. Keep in mind, depending on your culture,
autism might be viewed as a punishment or something that
only occurs within certain groups of people. All of these
ties—interpersonal relationships, our own relationship with
disability, and our socioeconomic, religious, cultural, and racial
backgrounds—play into how we have these talks.

Siblings

I am an only child, so I am not exactly an expert on sibling relations. I sometimes wonder if I had a sibling, how they would feel about me. Would they resent that certain resources went to me because of my disability? Would they be bullied or treated differently because I was their sister? Would they expect more or have a complicated relationship with our parents?

I do my best to learn as much as I can about the experiences of neurotypical, nondisabled children who have autistic siblings. Research shows that the siblings of autistic kids exhibit a lot of maturity, independence, and empathy, and have strong problem-solving skills. But that's not an easy road, with some studies showing siblings experiencing more behavioral and emotional difficulties, and a complex, challenging range of emotions and mental health concerns to be on the lookout for (Sipowicz et al., 2022).

Seek out developmentally appropriate resources

I bet you were expecting me to say "age-appropriate" resources. I say developmentally appropriate because each child is different in terms of their maturity, understanding, and interests. Some might have far more knowledge than you expect from defending their sibling at school from bullies or criticism/venting from their own friend or peer groups. Generally speaking, kids of all ages are smarter and wiser than we give them credit for. You know yourself and family best, and can work around what you believe is their level of maturity and potential to learn.

Often, local organizations and nonprofits have sibling support or respite groups. These might be a great way for your neurotypical children and teens to socialize, make friends, talk about their feelings and struggles in a healthy way, and connect with people who "get it" and can validate their unique experiences with having a disabled sibling. Outside of that, there are ways to connect online, where safety, of course, should come first.

Do a lot of listening

Siblings often have different experiences and perceptions of both you as a parent and their neurodivergent sibling. You'll really want to consider asking them questions about how it affects them and their world. You might learn more about all of your kids this way, especially in situations where you aren't around, like school or other activities.

Inadvertently, they may feel a lot of pressure and as if there are greater expectations of them. They might have to help more around the house, be expected to accommodate and stand up for their sibling at school or extracurricular activities, perform academically, or manage their emotions more independently than those who are only children or only have neurotypical, nondisabled siblings.

Something I picked up from my research is the potential of resentment towards the autistic, neurodivergent, or disabled sibling. The neurotypical sibling might have to compromise more often, deal with heightened expectations, or be accommodating in ways that are sacrificial in terms of their own interests, wants, and desires. They might hear "no" more often for a variety of reasons, including the support needs of the autistic sibling, the family's financial situation as it relates to needs and care, or their parents having less time for them because of caregiving demands, therapies and interventions, advocacy at school, long-term planning solutions, and other disability-related needs and priorities. These issues might crop up more as children become teenagers and adults, with fears over how their peers will treat and perceive them, or embarrassment over their autistic or disabled sibling or their behavior.

Continue to carve out time just for them

It's important to be attuned to the mental health of your other kids. In a 1991 study observing children and young adults between the ages of five and 20 who had an autistic brother or sister, as many as 35 percent of them admitted to feeling lonely, citing a lack of friends, isolation from their peers, preferring to stay home, and also keeping their neurodivergent brother or sister company (Bågenholm and Gillberg, 1991). More recent studies show higher levels of depression and loneliness in siblings who have autistic brothers or sisters compared to those who only have neurotypical siblings (Sipowicz et al., 2022). Creating stability and a sense of fairness can help alleviate these concerns.

A lot of the siblings I've met throughout the years feel as if their autistic family member is often the center of attention or the family unit's constant focus, which can lead to them experiencing a lot of pressure, stress, and anxiety, or turning towards problematic behaviors to cope or receive attention.

Even if they know their sibling has a disability, it's important to make time to spend with your other children. Think about their hobbies, interests, and wants, and enjoy time together without anyone else interfering or relying on them for respite.

Advocating for your child at school—the IEP and 504 Plan

School-based advocacy is quite possibly the most important place to be advocating and receiving autism-related services if you have an autistic or disabled child who is under the age of majority or is receiving certain post-secondary services until they age out. Depending on where you live depends on what laws and policies come into play to protect an autistic student's rights and interests. In the U.S., a lot of these changes to aid learning are known as *reasonable accommodations*; in the U.K., they are known as *reasonable adjustments*. Accommodations don't change *what* kids learn in school, just how they learn it. They are adjustments—like being able to sit in the front of the classroom to avoid distraction, sensory breaks, or even more visual presentations of academic information—that allow a student with a disability to participate, level the playing field, and give them their best chance at success in school.

In the U.S., students are entitled to a free and appropriate education in the least restrictive environment under the Individuals with Disabilities in Education Act (IDEA). That means your child has the right to attend public school and be in the classroom that is most likely for them to succeed and be included with their neurotypical, nondisabled peers as much as possible. If you or your child's pediatrician suspect or already know your child is neurodivergent, you can kickstart the process for a special education evaluation through the school to help them receive special education services and form an Individualized Education Plan (IEP). If the school or school district isn't helping to begin the evaluation process, then you can get a private evaluation. These evaluations have a few key players, such as an IEP coordinator or school principal,

TRUSTING AND TELLING OTHER KIDS AND ADULTS

your child's teachers (general or special education), the legal guardians/parents/caregivers, a school psychologist, and additional specialists such as speech and language.

Upon a successful evaluation, IEPs are created. An IEP is a collection of documents that detail a student's strengths, weaknesses, and goals. The spirit of an IEP is to meet a student's unique needs so they can be successful. The objectives should be ambitious, rather than the bare minimum or simply to be watched and babysat in a classroom at school. In 2017 in *Endrew F. v. Douglas County School District*, the U.S. Supreme Court ruled that an IEP has to at least allow students to make "appropriately ambitious" progress and provide more than *de minimis*—basically, the "appropriate" part of the education provided is key.

This is where advocacy, disclosure, and being proactive as a caregiver are important since you and your student have rights under the IEP process. Depending on the school district, there must be at least one IEP meeting to update and create the documents needed once every academic year, and the very first meeting needs to take place within 30 days of determining that the child is eligible for special education services.

Advocacy at IEP meetings is paramount. IEP meetings can be incredibly intimidating because of who is required to be there—in addition to you (and perhaps your autistic student if they are old enough or understand why they are there), special and general education teachers, someone from the school district, an expert like a school psychologist, teacher, or guidance counselor, and an interpreter if needed. Sometimes, specialists like speech and occupational therapists might be there as well. All of this can be scary when the professionals use a lot of language that might be exclusionary or go over your head.

However, you know the child best and their needs inside and outside of the classroom, to keep disclosing and advocating based on their behaviors and struggles that translate from the classroom to home. You know if they are struggling with homework, or if receiving speech and occupational therapy or other interventions during the school day would be of help. You may also hire a professional advocate or lawyer to make sure you're protecting your child's civil rights.

Under Section 504 of the Rehabilitation Act, students with disabilities are entitled to civil rights protections and the support they need to protect them from discrimination. Section 504 of the Rehabilitation Act covers any school that receives federal funding, so this can apply not just to public schools (IDEA only applies to public schools), but also to private and charter schools that receive money directly from the federal government and even private schools receiving funding from nonprofits that receive federal funding. Because it is not streamlined the same way public schools and special education are, there is no one "look" or governing ideal of what accommodations and 504 Plans to implement them will be like. Students will be in regular classrooms rather than special education classrooms. 504 Plans are not necessarily the same as receiving special education services but both require a determination that the student is eligible for accommodations. However, getting to this stage in the first place does require that you disclose and advocate for your child with a disability in order to receive supports in school. Accommodations under a 504 Plan can include standardized testing and classroom accommodations, and rather than having mandated meetings with specific people like an IEP meeting, each school handles the creation and oversight of a 504 Plan differently—some have annual meetings and involve a team, while others may be more informal. It's up to you as a caregiver to be your child's best advocate and to ensure they're getting the support they need to be academically and socially successful, especially without the same, predictable processes of going through IEP stuff in public schools.

If you're looking for more information and details on the IEP and 504 processes, one of my favorite resources is Understood (www.understood.org), which is geared towards providing information and resources to help people with learning and thinking differences to be successful in work, school, and life.

One thing I like to point out about both IEP and 504 meetings (while they are not the exact same thing) is to *include the student/child whenever possible*. When I first learned about my diagnosis at nine years old, I was immediately included in the equivalent of these meetings. Each year, before school started, my parents would meet with my teachers to discuss my autism and my needs and goals to be successful at school that upcoming academic year. I would meet my main teacher and we would all talk about what we hoped I'd accomplish over the year. I was academically gifted and earned good grades, so some years assigning more challenging reading and math was part of my plan. In fourth grade, when I was asked what I wanted that school year, my goal was very simple: to make friends with girls. All of my friends throughout elementary school were boys because I had similar interests—I played video games and traded Pokémon and Yu-Gi-Oh! cards with them, and I preferred action figures to dolls. I also was regularly excluded by the girls, but thought making some new friends would be good for me. My teacher and everyone else encouraged and listened to me when I shared how I wanted female friends. That was written into the plan. On the first day of school, I was seated next to a new female student, and all the adults helped me do my best to befriend her by pairing us up on projects and motivating us to socialize with each other. It was successful enough that when she brought her pet hermit crabs to school one day, she let me hold them, although I was scared out of my mind and hated the sensation of their little legs poking the palm of my hand. Disclosure helped me advocate for myself enough to get the ball rolling to make that new friend to begin with, because I certainly could not have done that without the help of the adults in my life to support the process.

Outside of the U.S., students are also entitled to accommodations and adjustments to help them learn. In the United Kingdom, educators have to make reasonable adjustments for disabled pupils to make sure students with disabilities are not discriminated against. Publicly funded nurseries and schools, have to do their part to identify students with special educational needs and disabilities (SEN). If you have a child who you suspect has SEN, it's up to you to reach out to the nursery or school's special educational needs coordinator (SENCO). Thanks to this type of advocacy, your child may be eligible to receive special educational needs support like speech or occupational therapy during school, or an education, health, and care plan (EHC Plan) for those who may need more support than SEN regularly provides and are under the age of 25. Young people can only request their own EHC assessment if they are between 16 and 25 years old, so it falls on you to get this started with your local authority.

These types of assessments and evaluations help qualify

young people for reasonable adjustments. *Reasonable adjustments* mitigate disadvantages that disabled students have under the Equality Act, and schools have to work alongside the family, student, and other professionals involved to agree to necessary support.

All of these processes rely on parent advocacy, and suspicions, identifications, and disclosure lead to an uptick in services to allow your child to receive necessary support in school. In addition, it sets them up for the future when they are in post-secondary education—like a trade school, skills program, college, or university setting—to be able to advocate for themselves or have a history of supports to help implement current and future supports. As caregivers and family members, you likely know your young person best and how they learn, socialize, and what they will need in order to succeed at school. Sharing and advocating for them from a disability perspective can ensure they get an education where they are supported and have their unique needs met while also being challenged towards growth.

Advocacy in healthcare

Going to a doctor's office for any reason can be scary, and disclosing, like all situations, can feel like yet another form of mental gymnastics whether you are a patient or accompanying an autistic patient. Disclosure may lead to negative treatment and stereotyping. These fears are valid since research suggests physicians regularly underestimate the quality of life for people with disabilities (Crossley, 2017). Ableism in healthcare is pervasive.

On the flip side, disclosure can help build trust between the doctor and patient and allow an autistic patient to receive reasonable accommodations to make appointments and procedures less overwhelming. Disclosing in healthcare settings should be safe since doctors, nurses, and assistants should not make fun of autistic patients or deny them accommodations that might make the appointment doable for them, including but not limited to telehealth options, bringing a support person, having sensory aids, using plain language, or written communication.

Disclosing autism to doctors is probably one of my least favorite scenarios of all time, but for parents of children under 18 or for those who attend medical and healthcare appointments as a support person or legal guardian for disabled adults, it can be an absolute necessity. This is one of the few situations in which it might be pertinent to override personal preferences and disclose because autism is related to the person's medical history and can help chart the course of care being received.

Of course, there are exceptions to when you or your autistic child might not want medical professionals to know because of certain potential consequences. If you fear ableism might be a part of your loved one's appointment, make sure to be ready to advocate as best you can. Patients should be treated with care, respect, and dignity no matter who they are. If the disability is not relevant to the patient's care or they don't want to disclose it at an appointment outside of a medical history, respect that decision and know it might be to your advantage in order to get the proper care. There have been instances where disclosing was a hindrance to care because the physicians and nurses began asking me questions to assist other autistic patients, questioned my competence, or made extra notes in their charts in ways that made me regret bringing it up at all—or, worse, the accommodation requests I'd made were wholly ignored and I had to find new care providers. One exception that is a "must" for families disclosing if your neurodivergent child is under the age of 18, and has a formal diagnosis or is in the process of receiving one, is seeing a pediatrician, especially if your child is still young. A pediatrician can keep their eyes peeled for whether various developmental milestones are being reached and be able to point you in the right direction to resources to support your child's growth. After all, most forms of neurodivergence (and autism) are *developmental* disabilities that have traits that begin to appear at the toddler stage.

One good practice is being or bringing a support person (that's you if your child is still a minor or an adult who has asked or consented for you to be there) who can help fill out forms, understand and remember what happened during the appointment, and guide appointments in the right direction (such as "We're here for a checkup"). I like bringing my mom because I have a tendency to underestimate pain or discomfort or not notice certain symptoms. I can get overwhelmed after the cognitive demands of completing too many questionnaires and rattling off insurance information before even having met with the doctor. Typically, before appointments, I try to make a list of things I'd like to talk about during an appointment so I don't forget or have that info on hand if I can't take a support person with me. Due to executive functioning challenges, I might forget that list; if an appointment was last-minute due to an emergency or sudden illness or medical need, I might not have made a list in the first place.

All of these things are supposed to be safeguards to make disclosure and appointments run smoothly. However, despite being a pretty much independent adult woman, providers will often direct their questions to my mom rather than me and suddenly I feel invisible and uncomfortable. If you are a support person or parent and things are being directed at you that perhaps you're not the best authority on or the patient is able to answer and consent to themselves ("How is Johnny feeling today?"), you can gently point the provider to ask the question to the person themselves ("I think it might be best to ask Johnny how he is feeling") or turn to them and ask yourself ("Johnny, can you tell the doctor how you're feeling today?"). Sure, there are things only you can do if you're the legal guardian or there with a minor, such as consent to immunizations and tests, but basic questions can open the door to self-advocacy and give tools to allow autistics to feel seen and heard in their own care conversations.

However, it is important that healthcare personnel really listen to and *respect the patient* if you are accompanying the patient to appointments! As the caregiver, you are not the patient. What you want and need may not be the same as what the autistic person wants and needs. I come from legal practice, and even when we would work with minors or clients with disabilities who were considered incapacitated under the law, I would regularly have to remind other lawyers on the case that the minor or disabled person was the client, not their parent, guardian, or other support person who would come to the law office alongside them.

The same is true for healthcare. Remember, physicians have a professional responsibility to treat patients of all abilities with respect.

Community inclusion, activities, and disclosure

Sometimes, the main motivator for disclosure is inclusion and advocacy in activities and community participation. You want your child to be able to join in at clubs, recreational sports, or religious services, and you want to find the best time to go to a restaurant that will minimize the loud noises or bustling people. All of these might be great situations for disclosure, because the motivation ultimately boils down to *accommodation*. How can autistic people be meaningfully included and accommodated if people don't know we're autistic or how to best accommodate us or the strategies we're bringing along with us?

Nancy Popkin at the Autism Society of North Carolina considers community activity participation as "active disclosure," where you tell decision makers and organizers ahead of time (ideally) to have patience, understanding, and accommodations in a specific setting, which enables the autistic person to be more successful in that situation (Popkin, 2019). She gives the example of a young child attending a story time at a local library:

My child loves hearing stories and being around other children. But I wanted you to know that my child has autism. I will bring a mat to help her know where to sit, and she will be holding a fidget to help her focus. She may get up to move around. Just know that she is not intentionally being rude and will still be enjoying the story time, even if she doesn't seem to be paying attention. I will be present to support her as well. Thank you so much for your understanding. (Popkin, 2019)

I particularly like this disclosure example a lot since while the parent is not asking for a specific accommodation, the parent is aware of how their child may be perceived and has a game plan by being present and giving direction on where to sit as well as bringing a fidget to help with focus and sensory input. This might not be a necessary disclosure, but it is a proactive one that allows the people running the event to know how to be supportive or, at the very least, be nonjudgmental and enable the child's participation and inclusion at storytime. It wasn't necessary to explain too much about what autism is or is not, just how it may affect that specific situation through the child's movement and that she might be fidgeting a lot. Either way, I found it very matter-of-fact and informative, and it gives the right amount of heads-up without feeling overwhelming to the other person and helps avoid a negative reaction.

We did something similar to this when I was a teenager. One of my friends invited me to Universal Studios for her sixteenth birthday when the Harry Potter universe within the park first opened. My friend knew I was autistic, but her family did not, nor did they realize that taking and including me on this two-night trip might come with more needs and responsibilities than if they were bringing along a neurotypical teen. So, to prepare, my mom had a conversation with my friend's mom to make sure everybody felt confident once we knew I wanted to go and accepted the invitation. We thought about what might be important to know about traveling independently for me, like what to pack or what to do if something went wrong or I felt uncomfortable, but my mom also thought that some things were crucial for my friend's family to know, to make sure I was prepared and would be well included.

My mom told my friend's mom I have autism, and that I

had never traveled without my parents before on an overnight trip. We took stock of what might be hard for me about the trip—particularly, food. I am a notoriously picky eater and have sensory struggles with trying new foods. To accommodate me, my mom and my friend's mom put their heads together to land on a place for dinner at Universal that had food everybody would like. We had a full itinerary planned to ease the nerves and make sure I had the confidence to participate. While my friend wanted to do different things, there were things her brother and other family members wanted to do as well, so I got to decide which attractions to take part in (her brother and I didn't want to wait over an hour for my friend to receive her wizarding wand, so instead we went on some rollercoasters she was scared of and I got an adrenaline rush from). We ended up having a great time.

Some people and places are more accommodating than others and may have quiet times or sensory-friendly activities scheduled, but those may not be an option everywhere. If you are preparing for an "active disclosure" for community inclusion, here are my best tips and ideas to make sure it goes smoothly:

1. *Find your point person.* Who is the decision maker or organizer who you will be sharing this information with? Why do you want them to know—is it for an accommodation, support, or in case of an emergency? When you know who this person is, think about what would be the best way to contact them and have a conversation with them.

2. *Take stock of the individual's strengths, weaknesses, and*

TALKING THE TALK ABOUT AUTISM

needs. Each person (regardless of disability) has access needs, or things they require in order to communicate, learn, or take part in an activity. What traits might make participating harder? If you aren't really sure, think about the person—what is their sensory profile? Are they sensory seekers constantly wanting to touch and try new things, or are they sensory avoiders who run off at the slightest noise or unfamiliar touch?

3. *Figure out how those "weaknesses" and needs can be met.* If someone might be overwhelmed by loud noises, for instance, you can decide whether or not to advocate for fewer noises or a lower volume, or take into account what the person will do. For instance, I might not ask for an entire program to cut out the saxophonists playing their instruments, but I might let them know that due to my autism, I find the sound overwhelming and will go to a quiet space until the performance part of the event is over.

4. *Have an open conversation, prepare for questions, and be polite!* I know sometimes people have questions for us and our families. Like most disclosures, try to be matter-of-fact, share what you feel comfortable with, and thank people for their time and understanding. Kindness in the process goes a long way.

5. *Have a plan if the outcome isn't what you want.* If accommodations are denied, figure out who the next point person might be who is in charge of an activity or place,

or if it is worth filing a complaint if you're continually met with roadblocks and exclusion.

Oh, the places you go! Travel disclosure for families

When I was a kid, my family did not travel on long vacations an awful lot. My dad's job made it hard for us to get away as a family, so typically we'd only do weekend trips around Florida, mostly to Disney World. I do remember a few beach vacations sprinkled in there as well, but I can count how many times I had been on an airplane before the age of 18.

The most legendary of trips we'd take when I was growing up, though, were cruises. We lived fairly close to the major ports, so cruises were ridiculously easy to plan for us since they involved a short car trip and no airports. They also didn't require immense amounts of planning, and typically we'd schedule them to coincide with breaks from school and to accommodate my dad's work demands. What made cruises so great was *just* how accommodating they'd be for all-inclusive vacations—if you were a picky eater like me, no problem! The waiters would bring chicken tenders, fries, and my favorite fruits, and they always had a wide variety of desserts. Now, some of the major cruise lines are major players in the accessibility and inclusion space—Carnival Cruise Lines partnered with nonprofit KultureCity to be the first "sensory-inclusive" cruise line, with all guest-facing crew (especially those in the youth staff and guest services) trained in the needs of sensory and cognitive disabilities. Families can also check out sensory bags filled with fidgets, noise-canceling headphones, and more.

Royal Caribbean International has a partnership with Autism on the Seas to provide extra staff, and the cruise line has its own autism-friendly initiatives on board as well as trainings for its youth staff. Looking back in time, these initiatives didn't exist, but cruises always had the ingredients for being an accessible option and a relaxed environment to vacation *your way*, whatever that might look like. No wonder it was and continues to be a family favorite for us!

All of this is to say that a disability or neurodivergence doesn't have to be prohibitive for your family, but it can be part of the planning process when picking destinations, tours, or even planning ahead.

If you don't want to talk too much or share more information than necessary, the *Hidden Disabilities Sunflower* lanyards, bracelets, or pins can signal to staff at airports or other travel destinations or entryways that you or a travel companion might need extra assistance or time, or to be patient and understanding with you. It is a voluntary program and tool to allow the wearer to share they have a hidden disability, including autism. You can usually get these for free, and more than 230 airports globally in over 30 countries recognize the sunflower symbol for nonapparent disabilities. Check online for a list of partner organizations, airports, seaports, and businesses, and how to join if that is of interest to you or your family members (I got the wristbands for free once at a community event).

Heck, you can even enjoy the many venues nowadays that have sensory and quiet rooms, including airports. They are nonjudgmental spaces that allow you or your family members to unwind, stim, and get a break from the hustle and bustle of the airport, stadium, or other crowded and busy place. You don't even have to say why you're using them—just come as you are. While there isn't a comprehensive list of airports and other large venues like stadiums that have sensory rooms or other sensory-inclusive spaces, it can help to do some online research to see if any of your destinations or local travel hubs have this feature or consider looking into getting involved with starting an initiative yourself.

For families, disclosure can come not just at the planning and travel stage, but also when visiting attractions and picking destinations. As an adult, I still am a frequenter of the Disney parks as this is one of the perks of living in Florida, and when I go to the parks, I apply for their Disability Access Service in order to make the experience more enjoyable and accessible for me. I struggle to wait in the long queues for the attractions because they are loud, crowded, and cramped, with lots of crying and screaming children that easily overwhelm my sensory system. To do this, I have to go on the website about a month in advance and request a video chat with an employee who will ask me (or, if you are under 18, the caregiver alongside the person with a disability in the same room) why I need the accessibility accommodations and how my disability impacts my ability to wait or participate in events happening within the parks. Then they take my picture, upload the pass into my account, and pre-book some attractions for my next visit. Usually, the cast members and employees are very kind, but it can feel a little embarrassing and scary telling a stranger that I am struggling. Meanwhile, these programs especially can make all the difference for families who think of travel and autism as incompatible. For young neurodivergent children, waiting in queues can be absolutely meltdown inducing and ruin a perfectly planned vacation. In these situations, disclosure circles back to the main goals of receiving accommodations and support, and is the way to ensure that happens.

Another very cool thing I discovered while out and about was the Certified Autism Destination program for cities and towns, which allows businesses and tourist attractions to become Certified Autism Centers. Last summer, I was invited to visit High Point, North Carolina, for two days to experience a Certified Autism Destination. I never disclosed I was autistic to any of the businesses, hotels, restaurants, and attractions I visited, but they had quiet hours, a sensory garden attached to the library as well as sensory-friendly story times, and one of the museums even gave us a bag of fidgets and sensory toys to take with us if we felt overwhelmed. I did, however, ask a few questions about the experiences and input from autistic visitors to get a better feel for things. While there, I got to go to a baseball game, two museums, and a few restaurants; I painted a piece of pottery at a locally owned art studio, visited the library, and checked out the university. Many of the staff members at these establishments throughout High Point had received specific autism trainings to be able to accommodate and understand the needs of tourists and customers on the spectrum as well as their families. It was one of those things I might not have thought specifically to look for, but knowing Certified Autism Destinations and Certified Autism Centers exist can help with your trip planning to find places and things to do that are fun and accessible for the whole family, while easing the anxieties around disclosing autism because you're surrounded by people who already understand and can't wait to welcome you. Not all cities and towns go through this specific process, which I've heard is a long one, but they might be partnering with organizations in their local communities to receive autism or disability training or have some other designation that signals they are accommodating and welcoming to all. My hometown did something similar, and seeing that buy-in and excitement due to the work of self-advocates and families is awesome and makes me immensely proud of where I grew up.

Telling random strangers

Every October on social media, there is a post or two that goes viral or makes its way through my news feeds. This post is usually about blue pumpkin-shaped pails that a child may take when trick-or-treating on Halloween in order to signal to the homes giving out candy that the child is autistic and may be nonspeaking or struggle with verbal communication. The symbolic blue pumpkin explains that the person has autism-related difficulties asking for candy and politely thanking whoever puts candy or Halloween treats in their bucket. The intention is that a diagnosis shouldn't stop autistic kids from enjoying Halloween like anyone else, and so strangers and neighbors don't take the lack of "trick-or-treat!" or "thank you" as being rude or weird.

Understandably, Halloween can be a challenging holiday for autistic people with potentially sensory-unfriendly costumes that itch, have tags, or are otherwise uncomfortable. Going out at night with other people and asking for candy is outside of the regular routine and can send confusing messages about talking to strangers and even walking around the streets at night (an activity I don't always feel particularly safe doing as I live in a big city). But it doesn't always feel right or appropriate to have to disclose autism in order to collect Halloween candy or be deserving of kindness and compassion. Some fear that announcing their kids as different to the entire community is unfair and invites more judgment than they already experience at home and at school. Not to mention, there are also plenty of times when the child doesn't understand or know what the symbolism is enough to consent to public disclosure such as with the Halloween candy buckets. What may work for some, may not work for others—whether it is a holiday where the routine and traditions are outside of what happens on a typical day, a community activity, or while you're out and about living your life. Telling random strangers about a family member's disability can be fraught with judgment and confusion. As a parent or caregiver, making that decision on somebody's behalf can be an invasion of their privacy or invite stigma and others drawing conclusions about your home life. If it is possible, have regular family meetings to discuss boundaries and figure out where to draw the line when it comes to strangers and disclosure. It's good to be on the same page about major life decisions between caregivers, family members, and the person themselves if possible.

Sometimes, however, safety is the primary concern. If a child is having a meltdown in public and their safety and well-being are at risk, I would disclose on their behalf regardless of personal preference. Disclosure can be the best way to prevent well-meaning strangers from making a stressful situation even more complicated, or prevent a potentially traumatic or violent occurrence if law enforcement gets involved. Bystanders can and often do misinterpret autistic responses to overstimulation in public places as mental health crises. To plan for situations like these, I recommend coming up with a *family safety and crisis plan* at a separate time when everybody is calm and collected to discuss what to do in case of meltdowns and shutdowns in public, including when and how to share that it is related to autism. Consider it preventative disaster planning. These types of plans are also part of your ongoing disclosure conversations within your family, and can include information about what to do in an emergency, who should be called or be responding to a situation first, and when to escalate to 911 or the police. Disclosure should be part of this and not taken for granted, especially since it can be relevant to somebody's care and wellbeing on top of how they are treated by others.

Sometimes, disclosure can take place through objects. The state where I live, Florida, has a law on the books that allows people with developmental disabilities or their parents or guardians to have a driver's license or state identification card with a symbol on it that identifies them as an individual with a developmental disability. Of course, this program is optional. It is both celebrated and criticized simultaneously. I don't judge anyone who opts in, nor do I judge anyone who opts out, as long as it's a decision everyone involved feels comfortable and confident with or can change if or when they would like to.

Some families and self-advocates find identification markers to be an incredibly useful tool to have, especially when involving nonspeaking or minimally speaking autistic people. Others also think it is valuable for interactions with law enforcement in particular given that one in five autistic adolescents and young adults will interact with a police officer before age 21 (Rava *et al.*, 2017), and that it can lead to more understanding without too much explaining when handing over their driver's license or identification card. Disabled people are more likely than nondisabled people to face police violence or heightened suspicion, and having an extra disclosure tool can guide police officers and first responders to treat autistic people with respect, dignity, and care, and ultimately to respond appropriately beyond the various levels of training on disability they may have received throughout their careers.

I personally do not want a designation on my driver's license stating I have a developmental disability, even though it might be helpful in situations involving police officers or healthcare professionals in an emergency or if I am unable or unwilling to advocate for myself. I don't only show my driver's license to law enforcement or medical staffers. Once upon a time, I had to upload photos of my driver's license for the teams at Instagram and Facebook in order to get verified. While that's a one-off, most typically, I show my driver's license as my identification when I have to verify my identity for tax purposes or even if I buy a bottle of wine at the grocery store to prove I am above the legal age. I do not want a cashier or clerk knowing I am autistic when they are only supposed to be making sure I'm not underage—what if they use my disability status to stop me from making a purchase that required me to show my driver's license? I don't want to be treated as less competent or face judgment in situations where my disability is not part of the equation, whether that's in a store or where there may be consequences such as having a verified social media account.

If something like an identification program or registry is worth considering for you and your family, have a discussion about it and weigh the potential benefits and drawbacks together. While it is not a good option for me and not something I personally would choose, that does not mean it is not a good option for you and your autistic family member to safely disclose to all sorts of different people you encounter.

Instead of something on my driver's license that can cause inadvertent disclosure or immediate judgment, I like to have choices. One thing my parents bought at an autism conference when I was a teenager was some little cards that I kept in my bag at all times; essentially, they give me the option to disclose to new acquaintances, strangers, teachers, employers, or law enforcement and other emergency personnel. The cards explain very generally that the person who hands it to you has autism, and that they may struggle with communication, stim and fidget, and move in unexpected ways, and to please be understanding. When I learned how to drive, I kept them in my wallet and the glove box of the car in case of an emergency and I felt I needed a safe way to disclose to a police officer (with permission to take them out of my bag, glove box, or wallet) if I was ever pulled over and felt unable to best advocate for myself. These helped me explain when words might not come out and I would freeze up in high-stress, unfamiliar situations. I did not hand them out to anyone and everyone; even to this day, I use them incredibly sparingly as just another option in my disclosure toolbox. After all, my goal in the disclosure process is always to be able to advocate for myself as effectively and painlessly as possible. There are other similar resources that allow individuals to explain their disability and include emergency contact information of trusted individuals, caregivers, or guardians on them; they are often free or very inexpensive to order—again, they might be a great option as long as you know how to use them safely and properly.

Disclosing on the internet

Perhaps the other side of the Halloween blue pumpkin bucket conversation is the more hotly contested "disclosure on a child's behalf" conversation—sharing information about a child's autism or disability on the internet, whether it is through social media posts, videos, or a blog. When I wrote in *The Washington Post* several years ago about the potential of oversharing online (Moss, 2020c), parents wrote to me with mixed reactions about my concerns for their children's privacy. There are different types of disclosure on the internet, you see. There are plenty of parents finding and seeking support as well as building community groups in online spaces who go to great lengths not to reveal any identifying information about their family and practice internet safety in the process. There is also a line that can be crossed when parents become content creators, bloggers, and documentarians and overshare information in pursuit of influencing careers, sharing wide-reaching messages about tolerance and inclusion, or even when a cute moment featuring an autistic kid posted online suddenly goes viral and ends up on national television. Stories of cute autistic kids singing at their school concerts and nailing their solos warm my heart when I read the comments about inclusion and the child's talent. Stories showcasing meltdowns and evocations of pity make me concerned.

When I was a child, the internet was in its infancy, so disclosure on the internet wasn't really a thing in my family until my adult life. When I was first diagnosed with autism in 1997, dial-up was slow, and social media didn't exist. Blogs were brand new to many people. Amazon still largely only sold books. My parents used the internet to find in-person resources, not to consume content and read first-person accounts of raising an autistic child. Not only that, but as I was growing up, my mother in particular was not exactly what you would call tech-savvy. There was no way my life was going to be shared with the world when internet safety as it related to young people was a primary concern on evening television.

As a young teenager, I was engaged on social media. I had Facebook when I was about 13 years old. I made a public Facebook page for my artwork and autism events that it would benefit when I was 16 and later rebranded it when I was a university student to be more inclusive of all of my advocacy. But my first public "coming out" about autism was in person, in a classroom, and I didn't really talk about it on the internet. I don't know if I would've had the same attitude had I been a teenager today versus in the late 2000s and early 2010s where viral videos happened on places other than YouTube. We were too busy posting about the music we were listening to and complaining we had too much homework in simple one-sentence Facebook statuses that still pop up in my Facebook memories from time to time. It was big-time high school news when people posted deeply personal things, like when one of my classmates came out as gay our senior year and received an outpouring of support online, later telling me that my classroom experience helped give them the courage to write about their experience.

A lot has changed since those days. Our culture tends to overshare—now, as millennial peers and colleagues of mine are having babies of their own, I easily have access to their full names and dates of birth from the day they are born, thanks to social media posts announcing the arrival of the new bundle of joy, and I am also inundated with photos of adorable little ones and know when many of these toddlers hit major milestones. Needless to say, it's a lot of information we put out there without much of a thought to privacy or safety.

Sometimes, in the name of support, parents of children with disabilities *really* overshare to the point I feel awkward having such access to a stranger's life. I have seen detailed posts about an autistic teenager's first period, or viral videos when an autistic person is having a meltdown in public, all of which can feel shameful and embarrassing. Sometimes they even have prominent information contained in them, like a physical address at the top of a food delivery receipt. Often these videos and posts happen without consent and jeopardize not just a person's privacy but also their safety.

As a teenager learning about internet safety, one thing was repeated over and over to me—things on the internet live forever. Imagine writing it all in permanent marker—even if you think it's erased, it never really is. Even if it is posted to a 24-hour, friends-only story, it can easily be saved, archived, and screenshotted for all eternity. Those posts about a teenager's menstruation or a meltdown can quickly end up in the hands of cruel classmates and lead to teasing and bullying, or one day be on the desk of a potential employer who can immediately judge a person and ascertain disability status based on their parents' online activity. An instant need for support should not ignore long-term consequence—when disclosing or posting online, it's important to weigh the benefits and risks.

Back in 2020, when I was researching about parents who may overshare for *The Washington Post*, I stumbled across a post that is no longer available from Jess Wilson, who runs the Diary of a Mom page on Facebook and a corresponding blog. Wilson now has two adult daughters: one who is autistic, and one who is not. All posts about them are shared with permission and pseudonyms. Wilson had one great rule in place to help decide what personal things to post when her daughters were adolescents—"If it were me, and I were 12, would I want my mom telling this story to everyone I know?" Chances are, there are some stories and moments in life that we wouldn't mind being out there, while others we'd prefer to remain in the safe space of our own home. Helping others should not come at the cost of another person's dignity.

To practice online sharing safely and consent around disclosure, here are some tips.

Start small

Ask if it's okay if you can take their picture and share it with friends online or send it to other relatives, and what that means in terms of who can see it. You can also ask if it's okay to post in honor of Autism Acceptance Month or something similar when it comes to a more obvious disability disclosure, and run the words and photo by them. Recognize that disclosure is sometimes deeper than "my child has autism" and go from there. Of course, older teens may have their own social media and share this stuff themselves, and then you can maybe ask if it's okay to share or repost what they put online.

This doesn't just apply to disability stuff. Even now, I ask people if I can share photos on my social media pages so that I don't post a picture someone doesn't like of themselves. It is a way to show respect for everyone involved.

Have internet usage rules for everyone in the household

You also need rules about posting about other people such as family members. That means kids and other relatives should practice asking for consent about posting pictures or struggles or words about other people. For instance, you might have an issue with an autistic child lashing out and venting about your parenting decisions on social media ("My mom took away my *insert special interest* and she's so mean to me!"); it may be equally hurtful if you write about how difficult they are in certain moments and events that might not be appropriate for public consumption—even if it's all behind each other's back (not cool!). I purposely try to ask my family members and friends if I can post pictures of them on my social media as one way to practice this, and tell people to show me pictures of me before putting them online if possible (I will usually say yes, but I like to be sure it's something I feel confident about too!). Think of having an "acceptable use and posting policy"—sort of like an agreement. Everyone is following the same rules to keep it fair and respectful.

One rule I have with everyone who wants to post pictures with me is not to share them until after the event, in order to keep privacy and locations safe. For instance, I don't want to advertise when exactly I and three other people might be on vacation or out of town; the vacation photos everyone consented to sharing would be uploaded several days (or weeks) later. It's a way to keep not just you as an individual but also those around you—and your property—safe.

Use the "How would I feel if my mom said this about me?" test

My parents are both on social media now. There are things as an adult I would be slightly embarrassed about if they posted, but it would be okay. But as a young person, I'd be super embarrassed if my parents said I was difficult or burdensome, or posted certain photos that felt a little too personal or were of things I might not want my friends or other family members to see. It's hard to figure out the blurred lines between informative, cute, or embarrassing and a full-on disclosure and privacy issue—and with disability, it's extra complicated because you may have an autistic person who isn't able to properly say yes or no. In such a case, you have to use your best judgment.

Things I, an autistic adult, would generally feel uncomfortable about if my parents disclosed in a public forum like social media or a blog or video include:

- Puberty—I don't think the internet needs to know about my menstrual cycle or when I got my first period and how that experience was for me. I'm all for reducing the stigma around menstruation and people having access to menstrual products, and there are fabulous resources out there to prepare autistic people with uteruses for this, like Robyn Steward's *The Autism-Friendly Guide to Periods*. I can't imagine being an autistic person between the ages of 10 and 15 years old (when most get their first period) and having my parents or other family members announcing that to the world, even if I handled it well. Looking back, I'd be afraid of being bullied or teased. Today, as a working professional, I'd be afraid of how that information could haunt me in a job search or among colleagues who'd discover all sorts of intimate details about my body online. I wrote about things like puberty as a teen author, and I think I would've absolutely taken a different approach had I known what I know now, though most of it I find a little cringey yet relatable and not too widely broadcasted.

- Toileting—this should go without saying, but I know that issues related to potty training and bathroom needs are real, especially if someone in your household is nonspeaking, has an intellectual disability, and/or has additional behavioral issues. I consider this one more of a dignity thing. If you are seeking support, do your best to protect privacy at all costs, since this can be super embarrassing and violating not just for the person having a tough time but also for other family members. Sadly, other kids can be relentlessly unkind, and I worry for siblings here, too. Kind of like the puberty thing, there's no shame in having additional needs, and I respect the intent of decreasing stigma and not contributing to it by keeping things quiet, but there is also a fine line to be drawn as to whether or not everyone needs to know.

- Meltdowns—this is a "no" for me in a visual format such as videos or photos online, but I know there are mixed feelings on posting and sharing about this. For me, meltdowns are scary, confusing, overwhelming— something that happens when my body and brain have zero physical or emotional capacity to fight stimuli or keep it together any longer. It's basically like a panic attack. I do not wish to relive those moments on video, and honestly, the focus should be more on the safety plans discussed (an uninformed person may consider a meltdown to be aggressive or threatening behavior). When meltdowns occur, the top priority should *always* be comfort and safety, since meltdowns are distressing for everyone involved and carry extra shame and stigma with them (at least to me, because I feel horrible that I'm that dysregulated plus I am making others concerned for me). I am fine with revisiting meltdowns and talking about them long after they've happened. Those talks can create support for others and help bystanders know the differences between a meltdown, a tantrum, and a panic attack, and how best to help someone without causing trouble or trauma. I was once a documentary subject and had a meltdown, and I was thoroughly annoyed that the filmmaker just kept the camera rolling and expected me to talk about it immediately afterwards, rather than putting the camera away, helping me get somewhere quiet, and talking about it later on when things were calm and the moment had passed—and, of course, the footage was taken out of context and made me just feel bad about how neurotypicals must perceive these highly distressing, personal moments.

As for my autism diagnosis itself, I do not have much of an issue with this, but I know some folks might. Even as a young person, I didn't feel any shame around being autistic, so I didn't really care, and even when my peers knew, they weren't necessarily kinder or meaner to me—it was mostly just a neutral thing. I'd also think about what your privacy settings are on social media to determine how far and wide-reaching the information may be. Probably cool with family and friends, might be less of a "yes" with a public blog or YouTube channel.

If sharing the information feels crucial regardless, have an "online protection plan"

This is the equivalent of my favorite neurotypical advice asker who starts with "I have a friend" when they are really talking about themselves, except you really, truly want everyone to believe you are talking about your friend and not you. I know there is information we feel compelled to share online publicly or within virtual support groups that can otherwise be sensitive or compromising in some way, shape, or form, but it feels vital to have that connection or share tips and tricks. If this is you with that longing, come up with some ground rules for online protection, safety, and privacy. Here are some of my best ones:

- Use fake names and try not to use identifying information about your family. If you must, try leading with "my autistic 12-year-old"; you can leave out identifiers like gender if they aren't needed for the post or group discussion.

- You can also make a second account with a pseudonym for yourself and not share where you live or other details to best protect everyone. Some of my favorite parent bloggers have names they've invented for themselves and their kids, and they only share what country they live in. This also helps to separate your "autism and disability life stuff" from "life stuff I want people who really know me and my family to interact with." I have used screen names for non-life stuff to protect my privacy, mostly when I've played video games online.

- Don't share what school your kids go to.

- If you do giveaways or want people to physically send you resources, consider opening up a post office box for correspondence so people don't know where you live.

- Cross out identifying information on things like receipts and boarding passes, such as a full name, reservation number, or home address.

- Post pictures after the fact from a vacation or event in order to make sure people don't know exactly where you are or when your residence might be vacant with no one home, in order to prevent potential crime.

If all else fails, you can always fall back on receiving support through the "I have a friend" preface. I promise no one will judge you or think negatively of you if you're asking for yourself instead.

Have ongoing conversations about what we will and won't share with the public and online

I began having these conversations with my own family in earnest once I was being featured in the media and my parents were often asked to participate in interviews (with this being a two-way street, we'd discuss whether or not they wanted to join in!). We decided that certain struggles were okay to talk about and share—for example, that I might have anxiety and meltdowns—or lots of pictures from my childhood where I was dressed up in costume for school plays. But we were less okay talking about, say, issues around potty training because I am a working professional, or having meltdown footage used without context. Those types of stories, while they may be helpful to people needing support or seeking guidance, made us feel awkward or uncomfortable about sharing in the public sphere because of the long-lasting implications.

Disclosure is not just limited to a diagnosis, but also, at times, the realities, joys, and struggles surrounding it as well. It's important to be mindful of that when determining what and how much to share.

Needs, wants, and desires change over time, and so do our knowledge bases and maturity levels alongside our own sense of self. Having an ongoing conversation about what is and is not okay to share in any context, can be a huge benefit to anyone.

CHAPTER 5

DISCLOSING FOR INDIVIDUALS
Developing Autistic Identity

I N A BOOK ALL ABOUT DISCLOSURE to other people, and for family members and employers and who knows who else, we can't forget about the number-one relationship when it comes to having a disability: the one you have with yourself. Being honest, reflecting inward, and embarking on your own self-discovery and identity journey surely makes it easier for yourself and for others to be accepting, and turn so much into self-love.

Disclosure as a set-up for life

When I first was told about my autism at age nine, I had no idea how it would essentially set me up for the rest of my life to begin to take charge, explain myself, and find a sense of community and support.

A few years later, I was 13 years old and incredibly self-assured for an awkward soon-to-be high schooler. I was invited to speak on a panel at the Autism Society of America's annual conference in Orlando, Florida. I am pretty sure the only way you could've incentivized me to go to Orlando and talk about myself publicly (as much as I loved theater and public speaking) was the promise of a visit to Disney World afterwards, and a few minutes of sharing my story in exchange for a visit to the theme parks seemed to be a worthwhile trade. Little did I know how much that day would change my life more than seeing Cinderella's castle for the umpteenth time ever would. The panel was comprised of self-advocates like me. I was the youngest one by about ten years, and I was the only girl. I was casually telling stories about being a tween autistic girl, and was asked about how I knew I was autistic and seemingly was so confident. "Confident neurodivergent 13-year-olds" sounds sort of like a mismatch, the more I think about it, given how much masking I was doing and how much I had yet to learn about myself and my autism. But the very experience of sharing my story publicly for the first time, and not shrouded in secrecy the way I attempted to tell a friend or two the year before, was revolutionary. It was also the first time I got to spend ample time around other autistic people, and having a sense of identity and learning some tips and tricks from the college-aged autistics was massive for me. They were open about their autism outside of this little bubble of an autism conference. They were self-assured and advocated for themselves; one even lobbied their college campus to allow their dog to live with them in the dorms as an accommodation, and I was in total awe (having worked in disability rights, I now know this dog was an emotional support animal).

Although the lessons I learned here might not have been as applicable to my journey as I'd have expected, since I did go to college and live away (although not with a pet), it turns out that meeting other autistic and neurodivergent peers who were slightly older, and who I was able to look to as mentors in some way, eventually helped set me up for life.

Disclosing in community and lessons learned from other neurodivergent people

One of the coolest things that has come about from growing up in the digital age has been the rapid growth of communities of people with similar stories, cultures, and interests. It wasn't until I began spending more time online that I learned about celebrations of autistic culture, and more about neurodiversity and its sociopolitical history than I'd have ever imagined possible. Thanks to the internet, I have made a lot of friends I otherwise may not have had the chance to meet. I was able to connect with other neurodivergent and autistic people, who have, in turn, become friends, colleagues, mentors, and folks I'm able to look towards for inspiration and ideas.

Sharing you're autistic, neurodivergent, or disabled in a disability-led or focused space is a special experience. It doesn't come with the same mental gymnastics and careful consideration of definitions and reactions the way it does in neurotypical, nondisabled, everyday-life scenarios. Sharing among people with similar life experiences is almost an assumption, a given, a simple self-identification with no bells and whistles, where saying "I'm autistic" has been more than enough before we move on to talking about interests and passions, or about coping with some of the things that make life hard.

One of the best lessons I've learned from disclosing and joining in community is how to feel infinitely less alone. It's easy to feel like the only neurodivergent person on the planet sometimes. With other autistic and neurodivergent people, sometimes I'm able to bounce off ideas and thoughts, wondering aloud if a challenge or quirk is unique to just me, an autism thing, or a human thing that most people don't discuss for whatever reason. It can make some isolating experiences feel infinitely less lonely and incredibly validating. A lot of those alleged "me things" turn out to be cultural touchstones or "us things."

And together, we've had better solutions to problems and challenges than an accommodation at work or in the community at large can provide. I've mentioned to an autistic friend before how I struggle to clean my house, and at the time, he recommended an app called TaskRabbit that connected me to people who, for a small fee, would be able to help me with various executive functioning (and cleaning) challenges, like organizing drawers, being a work assistant for the day, and yes, even cleaning my apartment. While it turned out that having a professional house cleaner was an expense I wasn't willing to incur on a biweekly basis, I did feel more empowered knowing this tool, along with some others, was in my back pocket.

I also learned from other neurodivergent people about executive functioning hacks simply because we were all neurodivergent and trying to figure it out together. Some have recommended programs and apps like Goblin Tools to stay on track and sort tasks. Others have taught me how to best chunk tasks and information to get things done, and to practice grace and kindness towards myself when I don't always get it right.

Most of the time, disclosure in the neurodivergent community is just an entryway into better things. My neurodivergent friends and colleagues are usually just that—friends and colleagues like anyone else. We just have this shared and celebrated culture and understanding because we know this piece of identity background on one another. Usually, we spend time with our various interests, hanging out and talking about life.

All of which would not have been possible had I not disclosed to others in the community in a way that felt natural and painless.

If you're looking to learn more about neurodivergent and autistic culture, there are a few handy social media hashtags to keep in mind, like #ActuallyAutistic, #NeurodiverseSquad, and so many others within the disability community. There are also plenty of influencers and content creators who are changing the game. Even if you don't want to actively meet new people, these personalities can almost serve as a "friend in your head" who gives trusted advice and is relatable. Some of my favorites are Jessica McCabe from the "How to ADHD" YouTube channel, Paige Layle, and Chloe Hayden, for starters. They are able to both entertain and educate, while making me smile and feel like there are always other neurodivergent women who get it.

Internalized ableism, revisited in this context: from self-loathing to self-love

A quick reminder: internalized ableism is the act of absorbing and applying the beliefs and judgments of the world around us at a subconscious level. Essentially, what we might hear from the ableist world will subconsciously entangle itself into our inner thoughts and opinions about ourselves.

These judgments that we begin to believe about ourselves can cause us to have feelings of self-loathing, depression, anxiety, and low self-esteem. These thoughts can make us feel like we are unworthy of the accommodations we need and lead us to not ask for help, communicate our problems, or speak up when something is wrong—or even when we are excited about something because we think it is wrong, weird, or will be seen differently.

If left unchecked and unacknowledged, it might turn into deep-rooted self-hatred and cause damage to our mental and physical health. Regardless of age or gender, internalized ableism can happen to any of us and be treacherous for our wellbeing. It is, at times, something I still struggle with myself, wondering if I'm asking for "too much," if I'm "disabled enough" for certain accommodations, or if it's better to not give others room to judge whether my autism is my entire personality (it is not).

Swapping out self-loathing for self-love can help us live healthier and happier lives where we can be ourselves openly and without fear. I know it is a scary thought; like anything, it will take time, and disclosing helps to ease the journey along with understanding ourselves and trying to move forward so we can be better in the future. Speaking from experience, it is often a messy, imperfect journey, but a worthwhile and important one at that.

One way to help with this is looking to others and being open with ourselves about our struggles and journeys; with that is disclosure. Self-hatred can derive from the thought that we are going through life alone and that no one out there understands our struggles and issues. It is very easy to feel like the only autistic person in the world, especially if you're spending a lot of time in majority-neurotypical, non-autistic spaces like schools, universities, and most workplaces. While we are each different and have different paths, that does not mean we are alone.

Just spend a little bit of time online and you'll quickly find we are everywhere! One of the best features that social media has given the neurodivergent community is the ability to connect with others who are like us and who speak openly about their life and hardships, as well as celebrate their joy. When we see other neurodivergent individuals who are open about themselves, it can help us reprogram our own minds and find support, tools, and tricks in order to help us in our own self-acceptance and disclosure journeys to be more honest and open with ourselves and others.

Another way to be more accepting here and untangle internalized ableism is really getting to understand what your mask looks like. I know what it looked like as a young person, but as I got older, I would sometimes struggle to know what was truly me and what was me trying to survive and thrive simultaneously, until I was so tired I'd feel like I had to start from scratch. Having masks in social environments is not a bad thing at the surface level as it can be helpful to get through the day and to survive, but when they become a 24/7 escape from who you really are, this is where it can become harmful. Take time to assess your environment, peers, school or job, and yourself, and see if there are areas causing you to hide so much of yourself. With a mask on, we cannot tune into our instincts and voice, which is an essential part of a healthy mind and body. But we also need to be kind to ourselves as many of us mask in order to cope, assimilate, and survive in an often ableist world.

Some of the best strategies for unmasking are reconnecting with our special interests and passions, and exploring ways to express ourselves in a healthy, perhaps creative, manner. Finding ways to express yourself can be cathartic and help you find parts of yourself that you forgot were there and can come to learn again. This can be anything from journaling, writing stories, photography, or art. I love to draw and do it often, and I think it is a great way to express myself while connecting with the areas of myself that I love. Sometimes these activities can help you express emotions and feelings better than words can, and often they are some of our best talents and align with our passions.

Of course, this journey is incomplete without self-care. We don't always get it right and it surely isn't always easy! Self-care means many things to different people. There is the standard exercising, yoga, meditation, or a spa day, but many of these things might be overstimulating or not an option for neurodivergent individuals. That is okay. Self-care is not limited to those options. Self-care can also be watching your favorite movie, having your favorite snack, playing with your pet, or doing a hobby you enjoy. When you are able to connect to something that makes you feel calm and happy, you can help free your mind, increase serotonin levels, and relearn yourself.

Finally, part of community building and unlearning internalized ableism is leaning on others at times—which requires a bit of vulnerability and feels terrifying at times. The world around us brings deep-rooted ableism, and it might be difficult to pull it out of us, especially if changing environments is not possible. If you need extra help or see yourself falling into depression or anxiety because of it, reaching out for help is never a bad idea, even if it is just to a friend for some support and a hug. If you want to look for a therapist for the deeper problems, asking for help can be extremely beneficial. Don't be afraid to ask for help. We only have so much that we can handle, and help can ensure we don't handle things alone.

Shaping your narrative: how to develop strategies and tools to best tell your story and advocate for your needs

Ah, self-advocacy. The one thing that, as people with disabilities, is essentially beaten into us since we are young—get really, really good at advocating for yourself! Consider sharing your story with others to make friends and new allies! If you don't advocate for yourself, who will? All of this messaging can get confusing and frustrating. Advocating for yourself isn't always easy. I am a lawyer, and when I was in law school and in practice, my career and existence were solely focused on advocating for and with other people, businesses, organizations, laws and policies, and obviously my clients. "Zealous advocacy" for everyone else was an admirable and often celebrated trait that marked people as great litigators and lawyers. Yet something strange would happen—I was a lot more reserved, a lot less willing to advocate for myself than I was for the people around me. Why was that?

It turns out that advocating for yourself is an awful lot harder than advocating for others. I'm really good at standing up to bullies, hatred, and decisions and things I don't agree with because I have a strong internal sense of justice. But there's something about advocating for myself that is daunting and scary. As a recovering people pleaser, self-advocacy feels selfish when it is expressing my needs and teaching other people how to best treat and support me. That might be my own internalized ableism talking, but I have always tried to make other people feel comfortable, and I didn't want to scare them by requesting too much assistance or have people think I am incapable or being too difficult or too much of anything—so I became a "yes" person, even if my body or my brain thought "eh, maybe not."

Expressing my needs and desires makes me fold like a house of cards and retreat into my shell. Having the personal responsibility feels heavy since it is a lot scarier telling people something personal and maybe getting a "no" or having my needs or feelings potentially invalidated.

Even non-disability self-advocacy makes me nervous! It takes a lot of courage for me to pick up the phone and call a customer service agent to receive a price adjustment or initiate a return to receive a refund on merchandise—so much so that there are times I'd rather keep the items or pay a little bit more than have to talk to a stranger and make my case.

A lot of the time when I lead self-advocacy workshops, I am asked about how to best talk about yourself from a disability perspective. I'm not sure if there's a best way to do so, since every one of us has a unique journey to discovery and self-acceptance. I also know as an early-diagnosed person, I have a very different life journey and story to tell than someone who discovered they were autistic in their twenties or later—I know what it is like having a name for why you're a "different" kid, or what it is like to be denied accommodations while in school despite my (and my family's) best advocacy efforts. That's entirely different from the journeys of late-diagnosed or self-identified people who have told me stories about learning the neurotypical social norms and cues to mask and survive from reading books and watching TV and later mimicking popular, well-liked characters, just as many second-language learners recall learning English from cartoons.

The way you share and tell your story is wholly yours and totally unique to you! It should make you feel confident and feel true to you. Some people shape their narrative to be that of everything they have overcome in life, including disability and/or ableism. Some people tell their stories in a way that simply is about highlighting their "superpowers." While you might think these narratives are great or that they fall in line with what's known as "inspiration porn," or the objectification of disability for nondisabled people's benefit, it isn't your place to criticize and decide what the best practices are for self-advocates telling their own stories. Stories are special and unique, and very individual.

Like any tale being told, shaping your narrative is a lot like writing a story. You have *who*, *what*, *where*, *why*, and *how* involved—the main takeaway, though, is that the way those elements interact with each other depends on the way you tell your story.

Who in this case boils down to the people you are sharing your story with and disclosing to. When I lead a workshop or speak to the media, my *who* is usually not well versed in disability advocacy. I am often starting at the beginning in a manner they can relate to. I was a child who screamed and cried at everything! I was, on the surface, a "difficult" kid. So difficult that my parents were often criticized when I was a toddler for what they were or were not doing. You know those children who look as if they are throwing temper tantrums when you're at the store getting groceries and you're in the checkout line, and you're silently judging the adults or actually criticizing them to control their child? I was that kid, and I wasn't trying to make my mom's life horrible when she was buying groceries; I was simply overwhelmed by the store. (This type of example is a way to garner empathy towards people they've likely encountered before, because most people have seen a kid crying, screaming, or having some kind of apparent tantrum or meltdown in public.) I use this childhood type of storytelling to get to what autism looks like, and the many ways families and autistic people are often excluded and ostracized while giving them information to learn and process in order to do better while bringing in the concepts of neurodiversity; there's a good chance most of these people have only a very vague idea of what neurodiversity is, so I don't make a lot of assumptions.

If my *who* is a workplace supervisor or someone in a professional sphere, my narrative is going to look awfully different from the "once upon a time, I was diagnosed with autism at the age of three" narrative. It's going to be factually based and brief to make sure I get the accommodations I need and do not waste another person's time. Pragmatically, accommodations are the main reason I'm going to tell someone I work with unless we are also friends and I'm answering questions or having a more casual conversation. In these cases, I'm thinking of how I'm explaining I am autistic, what evidence I might have to back up being a qualified person with a disability, to prove I'm entitled to an accommodation if they ask for it, and what is difficult in my job that I want to begin the interactive process with in order to succeed and therefore be better able to perform at my job.

What is the purpose of telling your story? What makes you feel it is a good time, place, space, and reason to do this now? Obviously, you're qualified to tell your own story—you're the main character! Keep in mind what your goal may be.

Where you tell your story matters. Do you do it the minute you meet someone? When you trust them? Over email, text, phone, or in person? You know your *who*, and maybe even your *why*, so those can impact the *where* that feels most comfortable. You'll probably want to pick a venue that feels free of distraction or offers some kind of comfort.

Why you're choosing to disclose and tell your story in a given situation is also a key factor in determining the best way to shape your narrative. Are you trying to inspire people to make a difference? Do you want to feel truly accepted for who you are? Do you need support to participate in an activity or social outing? Is your workplace discriminating against you, or are you struggling to keep up with the demands of work or school and need an accommodation? This might be a great place to start when putting together what you might share so you can work backwards with a targeted goal in mind: receive support, feel accepted, seek advice, inspire others.

How you choose to begin these conversations is also up to you. It might begin with making an appointment to talk to your supervisor or human resources at work (of course, we'll talk a lot more about workplace disclosure and accommodations later) to make sure the higher-ups have the time to listen to you and get the ball rolling.

You might just want to announce you're autistic to the world (I've seen this several times throughout my life), the way many people come out for the first time, share a name change or new pronouns, or how celebrities disclose major diagnoses in the news. If you do, consider if you feel comfortable about that living on the internet in a social media or blog post, and if you're prepared to deal with people reaching out to you with questions, offering messages of acceptance, or even reacting negatively in a public forum.

You might not even choose to have a conversation in the first place and your *how* might simply be a passing remark to test the waters and that's it, quick and painless. Whatever you do, it's totally up to you and valid.

Whatever your approach in writing and sharing your story is, make sure you know all your facts (which I'd hope you do—it's your life and your experiences, after all!). You can make a list of things you think are important for people to know regardless of the situation to make sure you're hitting all the high notes you don't want to miss. For instance, you might want to mention the name of your neurodivergence, how long you've known, and to be balanced have a few things that are positive traits (to you) and a few things you are struggling with, and even have some ideas of what you may need help or support with in case somebody well intentioned asks how to be helpful or what they can do for you in response to your perceived bravery and very real self-advocacy.

It can be very intimidating to tell your story. On top of making a list, you might rehearse and come up with a few scripts to assist you. As much as people may look down on scripting interactions or think it's trivial to quote things, scripting is a really valuable tool to use to advocate because it allows you to use words and ideas that feel familiar to you in order to get your points across.

You might also feel so confident in your advocacy that you want to go out into the community and do more with this, or you might want some help developing skills.

I have found that learning to speak up for myself is liberating and helps me protect my own internal peace. It is not the big angry conflict starter I thought it would be once I learned to let go of the idea of perfection.

Developing self-advocacy skills with perspective

If you're interested in developing more skills, you can consider working with a neurodiversity-affirming therapist or professional who can help you and arm you with awesome strategies and ideas to get that confidence, self-esteem, and scripting under control, so that you feel ready to take things head-on.

If learning more as a self-advocate is of interest, in the U.S., there are over 60 Leadership Education on Neurodevelopmental Disabilities (LEND) programs typically offered through a university. Each interdisciplinary LEND program has different offerings, and some (if not most) are staffed by individuals with disabilities to ensure a "nothing about us without us" environment and help us be able to advocate for ourselves and receive and give care in numerous settings.

To that end, there's also a wonderful advocacy program out there called Partners in Policymaking. While not everyone who learns to advocate for themselves wants to get involved in disability advocacy on the political stage, Partners in Policymaking is another leadership-based training that is geared especially towards parents and individuals with disabilities. Partners in Policymaking is a year-long course and program that helps with empowerment, leadership skills, education, and more, and it is typically a free program; if there is travel required for in-person sessions, your state might work with you to subsidize or reimburse the costs.

You might also want to get involved with other community

initiatives, such as support groups for people with similar conditions to yours, or volunteer at a local or national organization or nonprofit. You might want to share what you're open to in order to get more comfortable with sharing your story and skills—maybe you want to be a facilitator, speak on a panel or at one of their events, or just work behind the scenes to watch and learn and model others' examples. Not only is volunteering a great way to get some intrinsic sense of purpose and motivation, but you're giving back to the community and helping others along the way while also learning a lot, too. Volunteerism is something I speak a lot about in *The Young Autistic Adult's Independence Handbook*, as so often we get really wrapped up in online and social media advocacy that we forget about the communities we live in and are a part of offline.

CHAPTER 6

DISCLOSING FOR INDIVIDUALS
Disclosing to Family Members, Romantic Partners, and Friends

MY PERSONAL LIFE IS WHOLLY DIFFERENT from my professional one. See, I am very, very openly autistic in both my personal and professional lives, but my attitudes are not the same. I don't always talk about my autism with family. In fact, it's pretty rare that I do. We just have an innate understanding after years and years, though there are things I continually learn about myself and feel I *have* to tell my parents, like when I figured out that sometimes I struggle with interoception and that's why I have no idea when I'm hungry or full until my stomach hurts, or why I run water so hot sometimes that I end up with red skin. Or, of course, the groundbreaking (for me, at least) discovery that I am not the moodiest person alive or forever having raging teenage-level hormonal mood swings when they occasionally decide to call me at the most inopportune times—chances are, it's because

I am heavily dysregulated from travel, stress, other emotional demands, or body stuff like a lack of sleep.

Family relationships can be fraught. Although I am very close with my parents, I don't have a ton of close relatives.

Something I learned over the years is every family has its dramas and conflicts, or difficult family members. Some people may have entirely disagreeable views on disability, as though it is something to be ashamed of or hidden away, or a hush-hush family secret. Once, I was at a charity event, and a mother and her adult son—let's call him Jamie—were talking to me. They were telling me about his grandmother, who viewed his disability as a "problem." Both Jamie and his mom insisted that he did not have a problem. They were active community members trying to improve the working conditions and opportunities available to people with disabilities. The "problem," as they told me, was Jamie's grandmother's lack of acceptance. This was due to many things, such as her age, cultural background, and understanding of disability. Ultimately, Jamie stood up to his grandmother, refusing to speak with her and participate in family gatherings where she was present because he did not feel he had a "problem." Eventually, his grandmother came around and began educating herself and reevaluating her family priorities. Jamie is a tireless advocate inside and outside of his family, and while I can't speak for him, how he speaks with and to his grandmother is likely wholly different from the immense love and support he gets from his mom, his friends, his siblings, and the rest of their community.

As for me, my relationship with autism has gotten better over time as I learned more and can educate those around me. I laugh a lot. I smile. I am proud. Sometimes I am self-deprecating. Sometimes I am angry and frustrated about why I can't just do the same stuff everyone else does without a hitch. It is emotional, in ways that advocating at a medical appointment or at work would likely never be, when the nature of telling my story is more factual to achieve a goal and access rather than acceptance and love. After all, don't we just want love and care from our family and friends?

Sure, the conversations with my parents are wonderful, but all my interpersonal relationship conversations have had varying degrees of success and failure. Just look back to the very first time I told a friend about my autism at the beginning of the book and how awkward and scared and afraid I was, and then there are stories I will tell you when things went super well, and sometimes things go sideways. Let's go.

When your family is the last to figure it out: keeping your cool and having a talk

I am not late diagnosed or discovered. I had the great privilege of being a late-speaking toddler who got kicked out of restaurants and preschool, and received applause from fellow passengers for disembarking an airplane as a crying and screaming baby. I was enough to ostracize my family from community and social activities and was ripe for an evaluation if not a diagnosis nearly straightaway, leading my family to numerous psychologists and neurologists who would diagnose me with autism when I was three years old. Of course, this means my parents, grandparents, aunts and uncles, and older cousin all knew I was autistic before I did.

But what happens when you're the one who discovers you're autistic before your family ever does? No big family secrets of "we've always known" (though if this is the case, your many reactions and emotions, from betrayal to protection to rage to forgiveness, are valid and you should hold space for those and work them out with a therapist or other counselor or professional to assist). Just...you're the first one to have done your research and begun exploring or you have explored getting evaluated and diagnosed, or self-identified accordingly.

Depending on your age, you might have different resources available and at your disposal. If you are a young person still living at home—especially if you're a teenager under your parents' (or other adults') roof—you're going to want to do a little bit more homework and research. One of the best resources you might have available to you is your school's guidance counselors or psychologists, who can give you strategies and help corral your parents or adult caregivers/family members in charge into a meeting or discussion to help get you tested and evaluated. This can also get the ball rolling on receiving special education services of any kind, which might be the goal in the first place. Of course, this is all assuming your parents are a safe space and won't lash out at you, or you're not in an unhealthy or abusive situation; again, weighing your options with a professional at school is a great first step in figuring out what steps you might want to take. If you are already receiving private mental health services, you might want to bring it up with them. Or you can always mention this stuff to your family doctor or pediatrician (they don't just see babies, but pretty much anyone who is not yet a fully fledged adult or under 21) when your caregivers step out of the room (I know for a fact most times I went to doctors as a young person, there would always be times the doctor asked my mom to leave to ask me questions, just in case I didn't want my mom to know the answer)—these are usually the moments doctors use to ask you about drugs, alcohol, and sex so they can address your concerns and safety and accurately measure your health without possibly getting you into trouble with your parents. That might be a great time to say, "You know, this is unrelated to what we just discussed, but I want your expertise and advice on something. I have a feeling I might be autistic. I'm not sure what to do, or how to talk to my parents about this. Do you have any ideas or referrals for us?"

You might also need your parents' or family members' guidance in helping you self-diagnose to begin with. While doing your research on autism or neurodivergence, you've probably found out that many traits and signs of autism begin in early childhood. Not all of us have memories of our toddler days, or when we said our first words; I certainly don't remember much before being maybe four or five years old and visiting Cinderella's castle for the first time. You might also want to really look back hard at your childhood memories to figure out what kinds of behaviors, thoughts, and feelings you had. Did you flap your hands a lot? Have obsessive, passionate interests that you hyper-focused on and other kids or family members thought were strange? Were you a "good" kid who was quiet and never caused trouble, or were you unable to sit still? Were you bullied and teased? Also, now that you are no longer a kid, how many of these challenges and traits are still present in your life?

If you're still in the self-discovery phase, this might be your intro to launch into the big autism or neurodivergence discussion. You can very calmly say something like "I've been researching and learning a lot about autism lately, and I think I might have it." Then you might ask a question about what you do or don't remember about when you were younger, like "When I was a kid, did I ever line my toys up?" or "How old was I when I started talking? I have no idea!" If you have neurotypical siblings or family members, you can always do a compare and contrast approach, saying, "I know my sister was talking nonstop since she was four! What was I like at that age?" if you are pretty confident that you weren't a chatterbox when you were in kindergarten.

Putting together all of these pieces can help you have some facts to back up your discovery if you think your parents will deny you are autistic or neurodivergent—as well as a strong foundation on the condition (or multiple conditions) you suspect or have come to learn that you have. Having as much information about your brain as possible to educate and inform, rather than be confrontational about, will make it easier for your family to understand what you've learned and where you're coming from.

If you don't live at home, or you already have enough information to have the "big talk" and share this new information with your family, here are a few steps and tips to help ease the process.

Pick a good time to have the conversation

Identity is big stuff that comes with a lot of feelings. You're going to want to find a time when everyone is calm, quiet, collected, and has more than a couple of minutes to be in the same place and have a mature discussion. You want everyone to be able to listen and focus, and ideally not amid total chaos such as during a big life transition or over a major holiday, even though those times might seem easier because there are other relatives you might want to inform at the same time. However, it's probably best to have these conversations gradually, one at a time, rather than announce you're autistic or might be autistic at Thanksgiving dinner—though I guess if you're an adult and no longer live with family members, holidays might be ideal times to sit people down, knowing that if it goes poorly, you get to go back home after the festivities.

To figure out if it's a good time to talk, see if everyone has time and is available to chat, ideally in person. You can schedule this as formally or informally as you see fit. Or, of course, you can say something direct like "There is something important I want to talk to you about. Are you free to sit down and talk for a bit?"

Think of how you frame the conversation

You'll probably want to make sure it's clear that you're talking about something serious. You might want to say, "I have something big to share with you," or "I have something important to tell you." That way, your family members can grasp the nature of the conversation. However, if you feel it is appropriate and fits your feelings about your identity, try to maintain an upbeat demeanor. Whenever people have any sort of "we need to talk about something important" conversation with me, my heart feels like it will pound out of my chest, and my anxiety spikes. I immediately default to the impending talk being an unwanted or bad news conversation about to happen, such as an incurable illness, death, breakup, or something your family might not approve of like an upcoming or spontaneous engagement/marriage or an unplanned pregnancy. Unless you lump disability in there with those things, try to at least set the tone that it is important and serious.

If you are a member of the LGBTQ+ community, this is likely similar to the feeling of "coming out"—kind of scary, kind of nerve-wracking, requiring a lot of planning, and hoping for acceptance and understanding. And you hopefully have built a community along the way to help prepare you and that accepts you even if your family does not quite understand.

Depending on where you are in your journey, just say it

If you're looking for your family to help refer and take you to a specialist, you'll probably want to lead with "I think I might be autistic," and then, going back to all of the research you've done and traits you believe point to this conclusion, you'll elaborate and share more. Helping your family understand why you think you might be autistic is huge here. If they've lived with you, they'll probably have observed some of these things in you, or even themselves—it could unpack and explain a lot of things that just run in the family. It's not unusual if you have a neurodiverse family.

If you haven't formally been diagnosed yet, you might want to use more tentative language to show you're open-minded and exploring, no matter how certain you are right now. You might not be autistic, but you may be neurodivergent in some other way. Just remember, there is no one way to be autistic or neurodivergent. You may have ADHD or a mental health condition instead of or in addition to autism, so leaving the door open here allows your family to support you in receiving help for some other brain-based differences. Regardless, this can at least be the necessary push or step you need to help make an appointment with a specialist or provide you with some family-based context.

Think about how this information benefits them

Even if you aren't sure if your family will be very accepting, having information about your autism—diagnosed, self-identified, or suspected—can be incredibly helpful for them as well. If you have a neurodivergent sibling, it can provide further evidence towards how neurodiversity can often run within families, and set them (and you) up for greater support.

One thing that often happens when children are diagnosed with autism or another form of neurodivergence is it sparks conversation and reflection for family members, who may begin to recognize the same traits in themselves or other relatives. When a child of any age receives an autism diagnosis, sometimes parents and caregivers recognize that they exhibit(ed) the same traits as their offspring, perhaps brushing those things aside as individual quirks or "all kids do that!" when really they're traits that point towards autism. While there are no exact statistics on the phenomenon of parents finding out they're autistic after their children are assessed, it's hard to ignore the phenomenon now that diagnoses are more accessible and the criteria are clearer than for previous generations (Moorehead, 2021)—hence, many of our parents and grandparents were not diagnosed (of course, you might get pushback like "autism and ADHD didn't exist in my day"). Some might have even grown up when stigma was even more of an issue than it is today, where family members, peers, neighbors, and others with intellectual disabilities and developmental disabilities like autism would be institutionalized and rarely lived at home, within the community.

When family members have these lightbulb moments, it can be a lot to process, leading to them seeking out diagnoses for themselves if autistic or neurodivergent traits interfere with their daily lives enough to require more support or to provide a sense of knowing and peace.

These discoveries end up impacting the autism and neurodiversity landscape for the better—more people are able to access services and support, and it helps bridge the gaps between who gets diagnosed or assessed, meaning more women, older people, and people of color are being screened and seeking help—all populations and demographics that are traditionally underrepresented when the focus has been skewed mostly towards young boys in particular.

Not only can this information help your family understand themselves and your family history, but it can also benefit your relatives so they are better able to understand and support you. Maybe you were considered weird, didn't fit in, didn't have the same interests as your peers, and your caregivers and siblings didn't know what to do with you. Or, realizing that maybe this is the specific reason you've struggled with making friends or at school, they can advocate alongside you to receive accommodations and adjustments that will help you thrive throughout the rest of your school career and in life.

Give them time to process

A diagnosis or potential self-discovery comes with a lot of feelings ranging from joy to grief to anger to sadness to relief. There is no correct way your family will react, and if you're expecting them to immediately celebrate with a congratulatory cake, you might need to temper your expectations a little bit.

Autism or neurodivergence might come as a shock to them. When you chose to have this initial conversation, they might have been expecting other news given its serious nature, such as a change in employment, school, a coming out regarding your sexuality, a new romantic partner, or another major life transition or decision. Keep in mind this can be a surprise for a lot of reasons—they suspected it, they denied it, they simply didn't know anything to begin with.

Your family members might also feel guilty that they didn't pick up on this sooner, or were unable to provide for you in some way. If you feel it is appropriate (and true!), you can reassure them that it is not their fault, but now that you all have this information to hand, you can move forward to make sure you get the services and help you may need.

There are also situations where family members knew you had a nonapparent disability before you told them, and either they didn't say anything due to not getting you evaluated or they already had received a formal diagnosis for you at some point and chose to withhold this information. These situations can also be sources of guilt and may be difficult for you and your family. It is understandable if this breaks your trust or fundamentally alters your relationship—and not for the better. If this is the case, I recommend talking to a trusted professional, or perhaps finding a family counselor if working through these issues as a family feels like a necessary and smart option going forward.

Talking to my friends, and the many ways we've fallen in and out over this stuff

Friendship has always been a tricky thing for me. As an autistic person, I have spent my entire life trying to make sense of the neurotypical social landscape. The very first friend I talked to about my autism was in the seventh grade, before I had any solid footing in my self-advocacy skills and my own knowledge base about autism as a whole—and it was a disaster.

I was scared and ashamed, viewing it as a secret to keep and hoping the whole school wouldn't know by the end of the week because maybe I'd be teased or bullied.

Other times, I have had disclosure conversations with a trusted sidekick, such as one of my parents, who could help fill in the gaps of what I may have missed. This went particularly well when I told one of my best friends right before starting high school. We had a conversation altogether—me, her, my mom, and I think even her mom was part of it. We talked about what autism was, and I remember my friend and I being silly teenage girls and giggling while reading *All Cats Have Asperger Syndrome* together despite being self-proclaimed dog people. You might feel more comfortable having a parent, sibling, another friend, or even a professional help guide you through the conversations so they feel less awkward and someone else can support you with knowledge and things you may have initially forgotten to mention along the way.

As time goes on and my friendships deepen, I am also able to laugh about my autism, and so are my friends. I know this can take away from the seriousness of disclosure, but with a relationship that has a foundation in trust, respect, and loyalty, it's hard not to laugh now and then. It eases the tension, and it's okay if you laugh along *with* us, rather than laugh *at* us. This is great if you have a good relationship with your autistic or neurodivergent identity. Sometimes when we take a step back, we realize some of our struggles, quirks, and personality traits do have a bit of humor to them. I often tell people I have no choice sometimes but to laugh at my autism because it is sort of silly if I really think about it. My friends and family know I can't wrap my head around why driving and parking the car is so difficult for me when everyone else seems to do it flawlessly. People park their cars nearly every day and don't get into countless accidents in parking lots! That's mind-blowing to me. Of course, it's funny to others. On the other hand, there are things my family and friends find nearly impossible to do, like public speaking, while those things feel easy to me and give me an adrenaline rush. It's also funny how I notice the strange things people do, and if you let me explain, it's hard not to see how some of my worldview looks and feels a bit like a sitcom at times.

One of my friends and I trade Pokémon cards, and there is a unique way I like to organize mine. We have joked about how that very specific process—and my reaction to any deviation from it—is very autistic of me, as is having the level of knowledge I have about the series. None of this is meant with any negativity, and it's extremely clear we're just having fun collecting and trading through a shared hobby. For your friends, understanding what makes you who you are can bring clarity, trust, and even a bit of levity to your friendship.

If you're going "It's me! I'm the friend! What do I do?"

Chances are, your neurodivergent friend probably feels pretty vulnerable having this conversation with you. At least for me, I have a much easier time talking to complete strangers about my disability identity than I do to people I am closer with. I am less afraid of judgment from someone I don't know very well than an unfavorable reaction or discomfort from somebody I love or trust. That is the kind of rejection or negativity that feels scary—you have your guard down, and all of a sudden you see that shift in body language, that fumbling to find the right words, and you can't help but feel that there is a fundamental change in your friendship. It can be liberating or soul-crushing when we have these conversations. My friends largely are supportive, and possibly my favorite reaction of theirs is complete indifference. While this can seem harsh or insincere, I find that it is a relief when they are unfazed. They don't miss a beat when we have our first deep conversation. We just continue as if nothing ever happened, and they take their time processing this information and treat me as they always have. Sometimes this is a precursor to them being more thoughtful with genuine questions that I appreciate and don't usually cross over a boundary because we have an established foundation of trust and mutual respect. But generally, it is my favorite thing that can happen.

If you aren't one to be quiet and reflective, but see the need to say something, go back to the fact this is probably a little vulnerable and nerve-wracking for your neurodivergent or disabled friend to be talking about for a variety of reasons: their relationship with the topic or your reactions to what they're sharing. For me, I'm not nervous or ashamed at all about how some things are harder for me than others or that I'm autistic, but I am *always* anxious about how somebody else is going to react when I give them a few more details beyond the descriptor of "I'm autistic." Reactions are so varied to the point I have had friendships end over a disclosure before they even had a chance to blossom, or promising new friendships that began to unravel quickly once my autism began to affect them or how they planned to include me going forward.

One way you can immediately be a great ally is by realizing that any kind of disclosure, even a simple "I'm autistic," requires trust. You might not know why your friend is telling you this, or sharing some very specific disability- or neurodiversity-related struggle (example: "This place is *way* too loud for me" even if you don't think it's super loud, and then not too long after they say, "Can we go? I'll explain later..." and then they tell you later). When the moment happens, nicely tell them *you're glad they are opening up and trusting you*. Thank them and let them know you appreciate that in a way that's natural to your friendship. You might offer a hug, a comforting touch, or descriptive language, or just a few moments sitting with them to soak it in. All of these are ways you can communicate you are intent on listening and that you care.

Finally, *practice empathy and vulnerability in return*. I know if you are nondisabled or neurotypical, you might not be fully able to relate and appreciate what your friend is going through. It is vulnerable and honest for you to admit if you don't know much about their condition, or that you don't really get what they're experiencing but you're trying to understand. Here are some helpful things you can say that express this nicely:

- "I can see how this place is overwhelming for you! What can I do to help? Shall we get out of here?"

- "I will never know what it is like to be autistic, but I can only imagine how tough [insert situation] must feel or be for you right now."

- "I am really glad you told me. I feel like I understand you a little bit better."

- "At first, I thought you were just upset with me, but now I know you were frustrated that you couldn't express yourself in the moment. Thank you."

What works best for you in each situation may vary, but you know the people in your life better than I do, so trust your instincts on what will make them feel safe, loved, and supported.

For younger folks who have school buddies with disabilities, or adults and young people who volunteer with inclusion and friendship-based programs such as Special Olympics, you might have a friend with an intellectual or developmental disability through a nonprofit organization or school program. These friends with disabilities might have very unique understandings of their differences, either lamenting how they aren't included with typical kids or having high self-esteem. Everybody is different—and chances are, those in segregated settings, like special education classrooms or group homes or sheltered employment, already are aware and it's up to you to be a good listener when this person tells you for the first time or just straight up shares some details or vents at you.

Don't use neurodivergence as an excuse

Probably, one of the best pieces of advice I have for you when it comes to ongoing conversations with your friends is this: *don't use neurodivergence or disability as an excuse for inappropriate or poor behavior.* It can, however, be a great *explanation* for behavior. A disability does not absolve someone of accountability. Sometimes we disagree and face conflicts in friendships and relationships like everybody else. Making mistakes is natural. It is not an excuse to be mean, bully, belittle, or hurt other people because we might not get our way or be misunderstood. Leading with kindness and goodwill is key, and explaining when we don't understand something is totally okay. There is a distinction to be made between "Because I am autistic, I am typically very blunt. I'm aware my honesty hurt your feelings, and you found that rude, and I'm sorry" and "Well, you don't understand. I am very blunt and that's how it is because I have autism." We don't get to follow a different set of rules, and that's how we can determine the difference between excusing behavior, providing context, and still taking ownership of how we make other people feel while still having ongoing disclosure.

I have told my friends' secrets behind their backs as many of us have done. Gossip gets the better of us now and then. I know it is wrong to talk negatively about people behind their backs or to share things they trust me with that aren't intended for an audience beyond just me. Sometimes I did not know these tidbits of information were meant to be secrets, and it was only implied, so I'd tell another friend anyway. Of course, this has caused rifts in friendships and relationships. When it came time to apologize, I had to say, "Because I am autistic, sometimes I miss those unwritten cues. I'm sorry I told somebody else what was going on with you. Next time, if you trust me with something in confidence, can you tell me not to tell anybody so I know it's a secret?" It set the tone that I wasn't trying to be a jerk and humiliate anyone, and it also allowed me to take accountability and disclose in a way that my friends could provide context or it will fall on me to ask for it when they tell me something that feels sacred and special and meant just for me to know.

This same advice about excuses and explanations also applies to dating and romantic relationships. We will talk about romance and dating below, but I had to bring this up following the experiences of many autistic friends, particularly young autistic women typically at the behest of autistic men. I have observed autistic people engage in stalking, harassment, or bullying because of a rejection or an obsessive crush or interest in somebody, and immediately blamed autism for their wrongdoings. These types of behavior make people unsafe; unfortunately, they are prevalent in autistic spaces online, causing many autistic women and gender-diverse people to feel afraid. I understand not realizing your behavior might have made someone uncomfortable or invoked a trauma response, but often these types of boundaries are communicated verbally ("You keep calling me repeatedly; please don't contact me again") and clearly or in such a way that you could be aware (e.g. withdrawing from conversations or blocking your phone number or social media profiles), but saying it's because of a disability is simply not taking accountability and excusing bad behavior. Especially in these instances where behavior can escalate to potential crime or lawsuits, you'll really want to respect boundaries and acknowledge disability doesn't excuse you from having to refrain from your behavior, face consequences, or talk to a law enforcement officer.

Loving and accepting you: talking the talk in potential and current romantic relationships

There are a lot of resources out there for dating as people with disabilities, and as folks with nonapparent disabilities, disclosing autism and neurodivergence can be an especially difficult thing to judge from the get-go when putting yourself out there and meeting new people. This is even more pronounced because the most common way couples today meet is through online dating apps or elsewhere on the internet. How do you even begin to explain autism or a disability to a stranger in hopes of scoring that first date, or unravel if you've been masking this whole time and never actually disclosed?

Most people are pretty accepting or honest with their initial reactions. Usually, they share their own vulnerabilities and insecurities in exchange for the information if they feel a connection with you. Others are open-minded to getting to know you better and are grateful for the information.

Or they surprise you entirely. Once I had gone out with someone who admitted he was autistic himself on a later date after I disclosed on the first date. My reaction was probably less accepting than it should've been. While I was intrigued and excited, I came off mildly annoyed and upset that he hadn't told me sooner after I had already shared the exact same information about myself and therefore it was obviously safe to tell me. As a now slightly older and wiser person, I no longer feel that annoyance as I recognize the vastness of everyone's identity journey and varying comfort levels.

Try a prepared statement

To simplify the disclosure process, coming up with a short but succinct explanation of your autism and how it affects you can be helpful when meeting or potentially going out with new people. It's a scripted way to share information that can be positive while also setting some personal boundaries, especially with someone you haven't met in person before. You might say something like, "Before we meet, I should probably tell you something—I'm autistic! It's something I'm pretty proud of, but just know it's why I think we should have our first date at a less crowded place during the day so I'm less likely to become overwhelmed." Here, the disclosure came about because you want your potential date to know about how your brain works, and you also want them to be understanding when you're deciding on where you might meet up for the first time.

When I last tried writing a prepared statement for *The Young Autistic Adult's Independence Handbook*, here was what I came up with:

> You might just say, "Before we go out further, there is something you should know. It's a thing I explain to everyone I meet—I'm autistic. It means my brain works a little differently, I'm really passionate about the things that interest me, and sometimes I struggle socially and in loud and crowded places. Hopefully that's not a deal breaker for us." You don't have to give too many details early on, but just enough that you are able to get your autism out in the open and possibly weed out people who won't accept you for who you are. (Moss, 2021, p.101)

Looking back, I feel pretty confident about this as a prepared statement. It might potentially downplay some of your needs and daily struggles, but you also don't want to scare somebody off before they even get the chance to know you! If it does turn out to be a dealbreaker, then you are better off without that person. I say this because I had a match once who told me it was a dealbreaker and went on a horrible, ableist rant about a former autistic roommate of his and how he never wanted to associate or be around autistic people again because of how difficult they are. Good riddance. I am glad I didn't find that out at the dinner table or months later.

One overarching theme I've noticed in my attempts at writing prepared statements is a note of positivity. It helps break the ice and make it a little less scary. You can say it isn't a big deal if you don't feel like it's a big deal or will impact your partner too greatly. I tend to downplay if I use a similar strategy since I don't want people to be afraid of autism if I'd like to get them to know better, whether platonically or romantically. I also don't think my autism *is* a big deal. Among my friends, family, and even people I've dated, I often laugh about my autism. I think it makes some aspects of my life more difficult, yes, but it also brings me a lot of joy, and when you take a step back, some of the things it does in my life really are kind of funny. How can you not crack a smile or laugh at the fact I will naively miss the punchline of a joke, or that despite living in the same place for years, I still semi-freak out when my dryer is done with the laundry because of the buzzing sound it makes, and I should totally be used to it but somehow it always startles me? Exactly. Sometimes, a little bit of humor goes a long way as a coping mechanism here.

Let the conversation deepen over time

Assuming you got past an awkward first date or the process of getting to know one another, or you end up in a relationship with someone you were friends with first, your disclosures and conversations will naturally evolve past a prepared statement, a passing remark, or a self-deprecating joke now and then. Your autism and your idiosyncrasies will become a part of their life, just like their quirks and personality traits will become a part of yours. Your partner will observe your preferences, when you are seeking or avoiding sensory experiences, notice when you are anxious, or if you're unsure in social situations with them, their family, or others who know you both. One person I dated had simply looked up traits of autism in women and asked me if we could go through it in an attempt to better understand me. It was oddly comforting for me, since he was like, "Oh, I was wondering why you do this thing, and now I know it's part of your autism." It was an effort I greatly appreciated since so often we put a lot of effort into understanding the neurotypical mindset and culture.

As you begin to know and trust each other more, it gets easier and safer to share more with your partner. This will naturally happen, and it'll strengthen your relationship.

Exploring neurodiversity and a new diagnosis

Sometimes, if you are a late-diagnosed person or suspect you are neurodivergent, you might not have this information to arm your partner with from the beginning or to gently pepper in throughout your conversations as you begin to forge a connection. It is by no means a betrayal or withholding of information from them if you don't even know yourself yet. You have always been autistic, even if you and your partner haven't discovered it yet. You might choose to involve your partner in learning more about neurodiversity with you, or ask them if you display certain traits to help figure out your own identity. There's a lot of mutual love and support that can come about with this, and there are ways to introduce this understanding into your relationship if you are unsure, self-discovered, or seeking out more formal support.

It can feel very scary to say, "I think I might be autistic." You might choose to gently get to that conclusion or statement with your partner to assist you, saying things like, "You know how sometimes I am anxious when we meet new people?" and they nod their head and then you go, "It seems to be consistent with autism. What do you think?" in order to decide how supportive they may be or what their knowledge may be. Your partner may surprise you.

If you are a neurotypical or non-autistic partner trying to be an understanding ally, there are some things you can do. I learned a lot of this along the way through trial and error, and also from talking to some experts when I wrote about this for Scarleteen. Partners have had varied reactions, from complete acceptance and support, to indifference, to even disgust. Yet doing this "well" as an ally or neurotypical, nondisabled partner ultimately came down to three major things rather than being afraid to say or do the wrong thing. If you care and have an open heart, I have no doubt you'll be ready to learn and grow alongside your autistic partner.

Be ready for the disability conversation

Chances are, your partner will want to tell you at some point in the relationship and share more details. There is no "right" time to broach the subject as an ally, nor is there a "right" time for your partner to mention disability to you. In fact, this is multiple conversations that evolve over time. Just don't sidestep these conversations because you want to avoid having them or hope the subject never comes up.

Sometimes it comes up naturally, but I'd usually mention my disability for the first time in passing, and build upon my explanations as a relationship became more serious or if my partner came to me with questions. Someone I was talking to once was curious about certain things I did, like how if

I got excited, I'd occasionally interrupt to share what I was thinking immediately, and it made me sound like I didn't listen; he ended up searching online for common autistic traits and chose to point that out and ask some questions about other things I did and felt. It made us both feel connected to each other—I was openly answering questions, and he better understood me.

Sometimes, the conversation comes at the least opportune times. I had a boyfriend during college; it was a natural evolution from a friendship. We were together for a few months when we had our first, serious conversations about autism other than an offhand disclosure or two that came about with the "So, what were you involved with in high school?" talks and the fact I was working on *A Freshman Survival Guide for College Students with Autism Spectrum Disorders* when I would get home from class. One spring night, we went to a basketball game together. We enjoyed watching sports together on TV and were often too busy to go watch our university's team play at the arena on campus, but we finally agreed to go to a game. Despite loving the atmosphere, cheering, and school spirit, I barely made it to halftime at the basketball game. I felt a sensory overload coming on due to the squeaking of the players' shoes on the court; I was able to hear them loudly from where we were seated. When I watch basketball on TV, I'm able to take breaks or mute them if it's too much, but in person it's a different story. As the nerves were building and my brain was tired of fighting, all I had to say to my then-boyfriend was that I was overwhelmed. Without question, we grabbed our stuff and headed out. He walked me back to the dorms, and he simply accepted what happened. When I brought up this story to him more recently (we are still friends), he didn't even bring up autism; all he said was that it was the right thing to do since I was uncomfortable and no longer having a good time, and any decent guy or friend would've done the same thing.

A year later, we went to a J. Cole concert on campus, and I struggled with the noise and flashing laser lights. I agreed to go because I wanted to support my then-boyfriend, who really wanted to go and got us tickets. I didn't know much of J. Cole's music, and I wasn't a rap music fan, so I wasn't able to fight the stimuli as well as I had at other concerts I'd been to throughout my life where I was merely singing and swaying along to the music because I got swept up in the moment and my brain couldn't even process how loud it was until after going home. Needless to say, this ended similarly to the basketball game we went to—we left and went home. However, my then-boyfriend was disappointed to have missed a good portion of a show he was really looking forward to seeing by accommodating my needs, and I felt supremely guilty in my attempt to be supportive by going with him.

But something good did come of that perceived emotional conflict. A few days after the concert, we knew we had to sit down and talk about what happened. We talked about what sensory overloads felt like for me so we could try to figure out how to best avoid them in the future together and still go on dates we'd both find fun and accessible. It was a tender moment, and an organic, deeper conversation I had with someone I had known for several years at that point—definitely not something I would have wanted to discuss straightaway after telling someone I was autistic for the first time. Even though we are no longer together, over the years in no small part due to that conversation, we've been to countless movies, another

TALKING THE TALK ABOUT AUTISM

concert at a smaller venue, a hockey game, art festivals, and more. And we learned how to open up about mental health and neurodivergence in more mature and meaningful ways since we were 19-year-old students, which is something in itself to be proud of.

Another thing to keep in mind is *it is natural to be curious and ask questions*. There is a lot of information and literature out there on boundaries and etiquette when it comes to asking people with disabilities questions that can be considered invasive or rude. However, we're talking about dating and likely closer relationships here, where you're already in a committed relationship.

While there are questions that are understandably inappropriate to ask people with disabilities, there are plenty of instances in which the best etiquette is to ask, rather than to avoid. Asking thoughtful questions in closer relationships, like those between friends and partners, can be a way to show that you care about the person and want to better understand who they are (Ladau, 2021).

Validate your partner's experiences

I could tell you when I knew a relationship was going to end in a breakup well before we actually broke up. I had been dating somebody and was venting about some experience of mine that was, without a doubt, happening because I am autistic. We were on my couch, and I remember clear as day when he sat up, made eye contact with me, and said, "Well, you're just Haley, I don't see you as autistic" as I was explaining this very real challenge I faced. I felt immediately disheartened and froze up. I had no idea how to tell this person I trusted, was vulnerable with, and even thought I loved, how erased and sad I felt in that moment. It fundamentally altered our relationship, and, looking back, I regret not having the words to share how invalidated I felt. I might not remember what autism-related thing I was talking about that day, but I remember how deeply invalidated and erased I felt as I reconstructed my emotional walls. Unsurprisingly, communication issues and a lack of me opening up unraveled the relationship—the invalidation of my neurodivergence-related feelings and encounters only accelerated an ending.

One thing I have reckoned with in the years since that moment is what my partner could have said instead to validate my experiences, thoughts, and feelings in a way that continued to build trust and safety and contribute to an ongoing disclosure conversation. As we've already discussed, disclosure is an evolving, ongoing thing, never just the one moment when someone says, "I am autistic, and you should know that." As I think about my former partner sitting on my couch and holding my gaze, here are the things I would've loved to have heard instead of something along the lines of "Well, you don't have a disability to me" and denying very real struggles:

- "I hear you. That sounds really frustrating."

- "Is there anything I could do to help?"

- "I think I understand, but can you explain maybe why that's hard for you?"

- "I see you, I hear you, and I care about you."

- "I don't quite get it, but thank you for sharing that with me."

Even if the vocabulary and emotional scripting wasn't there, these phrases also echo the intent I'd have appreciated that would've helped me express myself and feel comfortable about opening up—even if a partner didn't fully grasp why I felt the way I felt but was prepared to simply validate and find their way through the moment. Making us not feel "othered" and accepting that autism is a part of who we are and how we experience the world makes a world of difference, and it makes it feel better when we have someone who cares and loves us by our side.

Even with a full toolbox, I promise you're not always going to get it right if you're an ally. I say this as someone who has also dated autistic men and felt like I had to learn all about autism as if I knew nothing from the start because their experiences were unlike mine. I messed up plenty, not understanding their sensory and social needs, or why I was more confident in my disability identity than they were. A common diagnosis or identity alone does not make for solid partnerships, which is the advice I'd give to autistic daters looking to avoid disclosure by dating other autistic and neurodivergent people who they assume will just intrinsically "get it." That is all to say, it isn't *if* you'll say or do something that isn't correct or will hurt your neurodivergent partner's feelings, but *when* you will. Even if you have no clue what a meltdown or sensory overload feels like, knowing how to get your partner to calm down or give them something they appreciate or enjoy—like a firm or light touch, a hug, or a comforting object—is a way to validate that experience in a nonjudgmental way. So is something like "I can only imagine how loud this place must feel for you! Do you want to get out of here?"—and not holding it against them if they do want to get out even though you wanted to stay.

If you want to learn a bit more as a partner or ally, one of my favorite disability allyship books out there is Emily Ladau's *Demystifying Disability*. Ladau says it's important to understand disability as part of a whole person, and quotes Sandy Ho, a community organizer, in explaining how disability cuts across political, social, and cultural narratives and identities (Ladau, 2021). Taking all of these things together—your partner's upbringing, race, sexuality, gender, religion, and disability status—can help you better understand them.

Signal trust and safety

Ladau also says that open communication about personal aspects of identity is part of the ongoing, trust-building process (Ladau, 2021). This also is when you have to respect somebody's boundaries if they don't feel up to sharing more, to know when is a good stopping point, and not to push too hard into forcing someone to open up when they aren't ready or don't feel comfortable doing so.

When I spoke with Amy Gravino, an autistic sexuality advocate and dating coach at the Rutgers Center for Adult Autism Services, while I was writing a piece for Scarleteen, she also was on board with the importance of trust and safety for both partners—especially since disability-related challenges are unavoidable. "We're going to have challenges," she explained, "and we need to know you're somebody we can trust and feel safe with" (Moss, 2021).

It doesn't matter how embarrassing or small those challenges may be, but being willing to step up to the plate certainly helps. I went out to dinner once with someone who had cerebral palsy, and they were going to send a dish back to the kitchen because of a lack of motor skills to use the knife and fork to cut the meat. While my motor skills are also not great—and I am left-handed so they are backwards—I offered to help. Going forward, this signaled that I wasn't afraid or ashamed of disability challenges. It provided a level of safety and support that was largely unexpected, but it was one of the times I was on the other side and had to be a good ally in return. Heck, one of the guys I dated even helped me straighten my hair for an event since I didn't have the motor skills and was afraid to burn myself, whereas he was adept with hairstyling tools from having attended punk rock concerts as a teenager. It was a little embarrassing for me to ask for help that evening, but I greatly appreciated the willingness, and he did a pretty awesome job, actually.

Signaling safety also comes along with trust and respect in intimate relationships, and also with consent to sexual activities that may be overwhelming or impacted by neurodivergence or disability. Again, this loops back to how everything is intersectional.

Good, intentional disclosure conversations allow our partners to advocate with us and give us the acceptance and support to fully be ourselves. Dating in general isn't always easy, and it isn't any easier if one or both of you have a disability. But it surely helps to have an amazing person who loves you and cares about you alongside you for the long haul.

CHAPTER 7

DISCLOSING FOR INDIVIDUALS
Keeping it Professional and Disclosing Neurodivergence at Work

NEURODIVERSITY AT WORK IS, quite possibly, everybody's favorite thing to talk about nowadays. It's one of mine as well. Navigating workplaces as a person with autism can be a little intimidating and comes with daunting prospects based on perceived power, bias, and inter-office politics. Some places are naturally inclusive, while others have a large undercurrent of ableism embedded in their workplace culture.

If you do disclose, there are protections in place to ensure you aren't discriminated against in the workplace—from the moment you send an application to the moment you choose to leave or are terminated from a position.

Regardless of whether or not you ever share you have a disability, your identity is perfectly valid. There are many reasons you might never share. You might not have the confirmation of a formal, medical diagnosis, and fear that you won't get the support you want and need due to a lack of documentation.

Again, that is okay—there are many reasons you might not have sought out or have access to a formal diagnosis or medical evaluation, such as your gender, race, socioeconomic situation, or where you live. Your workplace might be hostile, and you fear discrimination or "special" treatment, or retaliation if you report some kind of anti-disability action taken towards you. You might not feel safe or comfortable, or you are on your own identity journey and choose to keep this separate from work. All of these things are your choices at the end of the day, but we're going to go through the places where disclosure can happen if it is something you are open to doing and strategizing about.

Generally speaking, disclosure at work is viewed as a positive for autistic people and those around us. According to a study by Steven Kapp and his colleagues, neurotypical people regularly misunderstand and misinterpret autistic people's behaviors (Kapp *et al.*, 2019). Disclosure can mean that neurotypicals are less likely to misunderstand us.

Before we even get started: applications and interviews

Neurodivergent young people in particular face an uphill battle before they even enter the workforce. About 58 percent of young autistic people have work experience after high school and through their early 20s, and adults with intellectual and developmental disabilities (including autism) have an 85 percent unemployment rate (Moss, 2019b).

When you fill out an application for a job, sometimes a potential employer immediately collects demographic information on you, such as your race, ethnicity, gender identity, and/or disability status. Usually, this is stuff that the government requires employers to collect to show they are meeting affirmative action goals, and this information can't be used against you. In the U.S., organizations that are government contractors and subcontractors, or that receive federal funding, are the ones that ask this question for demographic data purposes.

But that question "Are you a person with a disability?" always filled me with dread, even if it was just for information purposes. There was the obvious answer—"yes"—which I was always concerned would be used against me or would mean an application went straight into a denial pile, never to be looked at by a person, or would open me up to biases. Despite being openly autistic in the vast majority of my work and life, this still made me nervous. The other two answers made me even more uncomfortable. Answering "no" was a flat-out lie and I am honest to a fault; also, isn't it bad to lie on a job application? The third option—"prefer not to disclose"—never sat right with me. It felt like a polite way of saying "Yes, but I don't want to tell you right now." When I brought this up to a colleague who worked in the Washington, D.C. office that oversaw federal contract compliance, it was a sobering moment, and we wondered if there was a better way.

Applications are pretty early on in the job process, and disclosure can be to your benefit, according to research. Wendy F. Hensel, a law professor and author of an article about the emerging legal issues surrounding autism at work, wrote that disclosure earlier in the job process can help explain when autistic work histories show "an inordinate number of jobs,

TALKING THE TALK ABOUT AUTISM

gaps between jobs, or a long history of self-employment" (Hensel, 2017). Employers can be thrown off by gaps and frequent changes in employers, thinking you are unreliable or disloyal, but autism, ableism, a lack of accommodation, or mistreatment might be the real cause. Knowing someone is autistic can help employers make sense of your history before interviewing you and not make snap character judgments based on factors beyond your control or your choices to protect your wellbeing.

To disclose or not to disclose: that is the question

There are many reasons a person may not choose to disclose they are neurodivergent at work. You might choose to avoid the conversation entirely for the following reasons:

- You don't want the perception of being treated differently or receiving "special treatment." This was always my greatest fear, especially since, at one workplace, I did get the equivalent of special treatment since my boss would always check to make sure everything was okay, and I'd receive more attention than my colleagues and coworkers would on certain matters. In addition, once a month, I'd get taken out to a nice lunch at a steak restaurant, while most were struggling to find five minutes to talk to our boss. The steak lunches were not so much about the food for me, but were a time we were able to get to know each other and I'd get asked more personal or sensitive questions about my autism and how things were going. I personally appreciated the effort, but I knew it left a sour taste in some of my coworkers' mouths, thinking I was the favorite or somehow being treated differently because I had a disability. The same also goes for folks who receive accommodations that others traditionally don't, such as a modified or remote/hybrid work schedule when it isn't so common in your specific workplace. It breeds a sense of resentment and can lead to workplace bullying or a less-than-accepting environment beyond just your accommodation solutions or supervisor.

- You have a fear of being perceived as "weak." Sometimes, workplace bullies or people who already don't like you might be looking for a "valid" excuse to justify their prejudices and actions. Disability is unfortunately viewed in many societies as a sign of weakness, and the wrong people will pounce on that, thinking you're somehow unqualified for the job. This was always my fear in law practice, where the opposing counsel and lawyers can and would sometimes make personal attacks against those of us on the other side, rather than representing their clients and criticizing the merits of our arguments and case. Disability could've been something my opposing counsel would pounce on as a reason to try to get me disqualified or invalidate the arguments I'd make in court, so this fear of weakness was one reason I didn't always want to disclose professionally. Lawyers also face and deal with a lot of stigma around mental health in particular, where dealing with anything neurological has a real possibility of being viewed as a sign of weakness rather than strength when seeking much-needed support.

- Concerns with professionalism are one reason, mostly rooted in ableism, that people don't feel comfortable disclosing. While disability and neurodiversity can explain a lot of quirks, such as an affinity for comfortable shoes, it can also lead to snap judgments about someone's competence and professionalism (on the flip side, it can absolve us of some of these criticisms, perhaps). Someone who is dyslexic might be viewed as unprofessional or lazy because of poor reading comprehension or frequent grammar and spelling mistakes, despite trying their best. You don't want people equating disability with lack of professionalism—that's ableist, and goes back to some of our earlier discussions about how society can view neurodivergent traits as moral and personal failures above all else.

- Concerns regarding professional licensing and qualifications are another valid worry for folks in certain specialties when it comes to disclosure decisions. For instance, neurodivergence and disability can be a dealbreaker for certain people looking to enlist in the military. In the legal profession, a lot of would-be lawyers are hesitant to disclose any neurological or mental health disability because of "fitness to practice," and these types of conditions raise queries about their moral character or ability to practice law competently, no matter how well managed the condition may be.

- Fear of discrimination and prejudice, of course, is a valid and real reason—if not the main reason—many people who have a nonapparent disability will elect never to talk about it in the workplace. While some may argue this contributes to a culture of stigma, personal safety and perceptions of safety are always something to take into account and respect. You know yourself and your current, past, or future workplaces best, and your comfort and psychological wellbeing come before any disclosure ever should or would.

Regardless of what you do, or even if you never say anything, your decision is valid and to be respected!

Neurodiversity at work programs: where disclosing is automatically in your favor

Some major companies actively go out of their way in order to recruit neurodivergent and autistic candidates in a variety of fields because of our unique perspectives, perceived and proven loyalty and productivity, and skills that we are known for bringing to the table. Neurodiversity at work initiatives of all sizes are usually fairly transparent about their recruiting processes, and require candidates to identify as autistic or neurodivergent up front to make sure the right people are applying and can benefit from the design of the interview and hiring process that is intended to assist neurodivergent and autistic people to succeed in their job hunt and eventual onboarding and acclimation.

If you're interested in learning more about getting involved or hired through a neurodiversity at work initiative, or perhaps even starting one within your organization, check out the Disability:IN Neurodiversity @ Work Employer Roundtable[1] and Playbook.[2]

---

1 https://disabilityin.org/what-we-do/committees/neurodiversity-at-work-roundtable
2 https://disabilityin.org/resource/autism-work-playbook

Other programs work with diverse disability talent, such as Project SEARCH, and many other private nonprofits and companies looking to do the work. If this is something of interest, consider connecting within your local community to see who is looking to directly engage with the autism and neurodiverse communities.

The real stories of interviews

Compared to neurodiversity at work initiatives, the majority of the job market is less forgiving. While job hunting, one of my friends used to mention she was autistic in every single interview she'd go on. Her approach was that she didn't want to work somewhere that didn't accept her for who she is, which is totally valid. It took her a while, but she eventually found a perfect fit where she's been ever since they made her an offer to join their organization.

As for me? I am in between a rock and a hard place when it comes to pre-job disclosure. I first began my job search in law school by looking at jobs related to disability rights, where having a disability of any kind translated to lived experience as an asset. Why wouldn't I want to play to my strengths? I quickly learned, however, that working at a disability rights organization full-time wasn't the dream I expected it to be. I would come home from a day at work, overwhelmed by the amount of empathy I had towards the disabled and neurodivergent people I'd be assisting. Their stories and crises would play in the back of my mind—some of them still do to this day. That heavy emotional connection steered me back towards the more traditional employment channels and jobs to be looking for after graduation—ones where I'd be able to have the coveted "work–life balance." But like many plans in life, my job search for my next summer in law school was quickly derailed when a chance conversation took place in an elevator in my apartment building. A lawyer who worked as a realtor at night was going to be showing the unit next door to mine and asked how I liked living there; I said it was convenient as a law student, and one thing led to another. I emailed my resume to him that night and had an interview scheduled at his firm for the next week. I wasn't planning on sharing that I was autistic before or during that interview, but a conversation with another attorney before my interview revealed that the firm's founder has an autistic child and my advocacy work piqued his interest. That made my interview go smoothly, and we had a lovely conversation, but it was also nontraditional in that we talked about ourselves and our families in a very personable, friendly way that required a certain level of understanding and trust. I had a job offer on the spot before I even left the office that evening.

But not every interview I've been to has been so empowering. Having a disability advocacy background means my resume is fairly empty if I exclude having a disability as part of it. I am immediately asked why I care so much about autism and neurodiversity. The last time I interviewed for a legal job, I was asked about my nontraditional background—I had law experience, but most of my practical experience was in other fields and talents as compared to, you know, the actual practice of law. I disclosed, feeling I had no other option to explain my passion and how my career took a turn in a different direction. Instead of focusing on the many strengths and talents I had learned as a former practicing attorney turned business owner, or what skills I had from when I was in practice, the interview immediately shifted gears into solely talking about my disability in a way that made me feel awkward. I felt dejected and,

TALKING THE TALK ABOUT AUTISM

unsurprisingly and to my relief, did not receive a job offer from that place.

Now, I know that isn't supposed to happen, and our rights as job candidates are protected just as much in the hiring and interview stages as are the rights of current employees. There are policies and procedures as to what interviewers and companies can and cannot ask without seemingly discriminating against us, though if we disclose, sometimes it isn't as simple as telling someone they are running afoul of the Americans with Disabilities Act since it's possibly in our best interests to tough it out in the hope of getting that coveted job offer. But for our purposes, here is a brief guide as to what employers can and can't legally ask about disability.

The ADA precludes employers from asking applicants questions that are "likely to elicit information about a disability."[3] To avoid eliciting information about neurodivergence that an applicant did not disclose, one of the first places to look to is the job description, which often lays out the essential functions of the job, which boil down to what the daily responsibilities, duties, and expectations are in order to be successful—not just the "nice to have" things.

Employers can ask you questions even if you disclose—for example, if you can do the job with or without an accommodation. For instance, verbal communication might be difficult at times for you because of autism, but if the job requires a lot of verbal communication with customers or colleagues, they might ask if you're capable of that with or without accommodations, and what you might need from them in order to be

---

3   EEOC, ADA Enforcement Guidance: Preemployment Disability-Related Questions and Medical Examinations 4 (2000); See also 42 U.S.C. § 12112(d) (2) (2012); 29 C.F.R. § 1603.13(a) (2016).

successful. They can also ask you about things like professional qualifications and past experiences.

However, even if you do disclose, employers can't request information about your specific disability. This happens far more often than not. You can decline to share if you don't feel comfortable, or you can try to play this to your advantage—if I'm asked a lot of invasive disability questions (that I know are potential ADA issues), I try to spin it and talk about the many life lessons being autistic has taught me or the strengths and skills and talents that I have, which my neurotypical peers may not have. In the same vein, they also can't ask you about your medical history, what medications you take, or if you've ever received mental health counseling or treatment.

If you do suspect during an interview that your rights were violated, you might look into filing a complaint with the U.S. Equal Employment Opportunity Commission.

Unfortunately, even with disclosure, interviewing is often a sport of masking. For instance, recruiters and hiring decision makers may view eye contact solely as a way to determine if someone is being honest. However, some neurodivergent people feel eye contact is a burdensome social convention that can be physically uncomfortable at one extreme or be the cause of long periods of inattention. For me, eye contact requires my focus to be diverted away from what people are saying. In interviews, I am on my best behavior, trying my absolute hardest to make eye contact, which leaves me feeling exhausted. I try to be as genuine and attentive as possible in order to put someone else at ease and convince them I am interested, engaged, and happy, when really my brain is doing its best while my body does something that feels unnatural. If I look away and fidget, that will be the only thing the recruiter or decision maker focuses on, especially if I disclose that I am autistic. Sometimes, they really are looking for a "culture fit" and how much a person can assimilate in an often stressful, neurotypical-focused environment that we aren't naturally designed for and which may ultimately not be in our best interest to join anyway.

But disclosure is not a lost cause, and having these conversations in interviews can also lead to some great conversations about allyship and disability inclusion initiatives in the workplace, and may give you an opportunity to highlight your journey of overcoming adversity and showcase your strengths. It is all about perspective, and it's almost impossible to bring about change if we all are masking to the point of burnout, even after we get past those initial hurdles.

Talking to managers, supervisors, colleagues, and clients

Your interactions at work are all unique, and each situation is different. Sometimes you might have a better relationship with a colleague, but harbor some fear or distrust towards your manager or supervisor. Maybe your workplace doesn't have any human resources professionals who can help you out because you work for a smaller business or organization, or maybe you're self-employed or own your own business and only have to interact with clients and contractors. Either way, these interpersonal dynamics can make disclosure feel even more confusing in your workplace!

The first thing I like to do is *find a person who feels safe to talk to*. Maybe this person is a colleague-turned-friend whom you trust, or a mentor who works elsewhere or within your workplace. This person might be great to test the waters with and bounce ideas off before approaching your manager, supervisor, or human resources people. You may practice a formal disclosure and what the purpose of that is, or how it may come up in passing, or when the right time is. For colleagues, though, make sure to set some ground rules so you know the conversation doesn't go further unless you're ready for it to do so.

If this safe person is your manager or supervisor, that's even better! Some people love their boss, while other people can't stand them. If you're one of those people who has a wonderful working relationship with your supervisor or manager and know they are good leaders who aren't judgmental, that should signal to you that disclosing a disability or neurodivergence is safe and that this person in a leadership position should be able to support you in some way, shape, or form. Be sure to have some private time with them when you do this, so you have their full focus, and you know exactly when the right time and place is if disclosure is what you're meeting about, or you may simply be giving them ideas of how to best support you or find out why you're hitting some roadblocks. I'd recommend ideally doing this face-to-face or on a video call (you don't want your written correspondence ending up in the wrong hands or being used against you somehow).

Talking to management about your disability can be especially helpful if you're somewhere that does annual reviews because that is a time when you give and receive feedback on your job performance. I recommend annual reviews since it's one of the few times you definitely will have your manager's undivided attention, and if you're too shy to schedule time to meet with them privately, this is an opportunity to do so, and the situation can provide some prompts and jumping-off points for a productive conversation. For instance, if an annual review reveals you're slow to complete tasks, that might be a great time to disclose and share you have executive functioning challenges so your manager can help chunk things to make your workload more manageable or provide reminders for deadlines so you're able to complete things in a timely manner and without feeling too overwhelmed.

I work for myself, so I don't have the added potential responsibilities of disclosing to management (I am management) or human resources (I have no other employees), or even managing neurodivergent employees or independent contractors. If you participate in the gig economy—for example, if you work for a rideshare or food delivery app—it likely will never come up with your clients. If you're a freelance designer or other worker, it might be relevant to your portfolio, biography, or an explanation later on if you aren't hitting deadlines or have an atypical communication style. I am very forthcoming because I work in disability and neurodiversity inclusion, but sometimes I have to share extra details if I'm behind on projects, need more guidance and clarity, or there's a disconnect between me and the clients I am assisting. Sometimes my clients are also neurodivergent, and we get onto a total tangent about joy and challenges, and that is an unexpected, beautiful thing, but not something I would expect to be the norm. If you're disclosing to work clients, *keep it informative and professional as much as possible*, sharing only what you feel comfortable with and knowing when it's okay to be more friendly and add in extra details. You don't want to scare people or inadvertently push them away because you feel too comfortable.

If you share with anyone at work, though, it's important to *discuss boundaries* surrounding this information. Workplace gossip can happen anytime or anywhere, and a disability, diagnosis, or granted accommodation isn't something you want feeding the rumor mill or becoming widespread knowledge if it is not already. Neurotypicals have a way of gossiping and speculating about accommodations as unfair advantages or preferential treatment, or trying to figure out what is "wrong" with somebody who doesn't fit into the dominant workplace culture. Depending on where you live, you may have some protection over what can be shared, since this can be classified as medical information. However, when disclosing, set some boundaries with your workplace crew so they know who they may talk to in order to help advocate for you, or discuss in general. It's totally uncool if your trusted colleague tells your manager when you had no intention of ever disclosing to your manager.

The Hitchhiker's Guide to soft disclosing at work for everybody

If soft disclosure—not saying anything specific, but wanting to improve overall communication with managers and colleagues—is for you, here's an idea. One of my neurotypical colleagues (who works primarily with neurodivergent people) has a Google document linked in her email signature that details how to best work with her. She called it "The Hitchhiker's Guide to [Her Name]." I find this amusing and a wonderful way to accommodate and work with her even though she doesn't have a disability. It's a few pages long and lists her strengths and weaknesses, and best practices for contacting and communicating with her, but it makes things easier and more inclusive for everybody. I use an adapted version of this with my colleagues and clients. It's only about three or four bullet points long and never mentions my disability. I consider this my version of *creating a "how to work with me" guide*. Here are my bullet points:

- I am not a morning person.

- Unprompted phone calls make me nervous.

- If you don't hear back from me via email within 48 hours (unless I've told you I am on vacation), please follow up with me!

All of these bullet points help explain the best ways to accommodate my brain and body. Here is why...

It's true that I am not a morning person, although that is wholly unrelated to my autism. I just value my sleep and don't want to appear groggy over the phone or on a video call, and I want to be fully focused without feeling too tired. Someone else who says "I am not a morning person" might be grumpy without their caffeine, or has children to get ready for school, or has depression or joint pain or a disability that makes getting out of bed early a difficult task. However, I sometimes have to accommodate morning people or people who are located across the globe in another time zone; whenever I work with colleagues in Europe, we have to schedule meetings in the morning because there is a five- or six-hour time difference (though we have agreed that no meetings should begin between seven and eight o'clock in the morning for me).

As for the unprompted phone calls, that is related to autism! I do get exceedingly nervous when people call me and it's unexpected. I don't know if it means I am in trouble, there is a telemarketer on the other line, or something bad happened. Typically, the only people who call me unprompted are relatives, and that's the exception—I know they just want to chitchat. Most others will text or email me asking if now is a good time to talk with perhaps a sentence or two about what we're going to talk about ("Are you free to talk in an hour? I really want to ask about the upcoming project"). That at least gives me a moment to mentally prepare and shoo away the nervous feeling that something is horribly wrong.

The email follow-up bullet point is the one I get the most mileage out of. My inbox feels like a black hole, and a lot of stuff shows up in there. I am the only one who manages my inbox. It is a lot of work for one person, and I don't always know what is urgent and what is important. My executive functioning skills honestly aren't great. I also have phases where I *mentally* hit "send," but physically do not, and your email will live in my drafts folder forever. A lot of people are hesitant to send follow-ups because they fear it is rude, but if it's been more than 48 hours, trust me, I'm grateful for the reminder, and it signals to me that your message is either urgent or important. The exception, of course, is if I'm on vacation, which is something I share with my colleagues and clients as necessary beforehand; that way, they know to follow up with me two days after my expected return, because it's likely I have a lot of catching up to do when I get home from traveling.

These things make disclosing feel safe without saying too much—you might not know why I need follow-ups or agendas or want things ideally to be scheduled slightly later in the morning or afternoon, but it allows you to accommodate my needs and preferences, as I will also do my best to meet yours. If we can't meet those specific needs—if something is truly an emergency or the time zones make it that we must meet early in the morning—we can work around that together. Some types of workplace disclosure don't just make it easier for neurodivergent and disabled people, but enable all workers to be better at setting boundaries and communicating with others.

Remember, when disclosing at work, it's important to figure out your *why*. We talked about this concept a little bit earlier when it comes to shaping your narrative and disclosing as a self-advocate to people you know, but at work, knowing your *why* is even more crucial and can help you pick the right time and place. You're already past the interview stage and have been working somewhere for at least a day or so if you're considering disclosing to colleagues and managers. Chances are, you heavily masked to get to this point, didn't disclose earlier in the employment life cycle, or didn't know you were neurodivergent (either unidentified or undiagnosed, or you didn't recognize your brain is classified as neurodivergent). Those factors alone can bring you to this conversation—you are burned out or wish to bring your true self to work in order to unmask, disclosing feels necessary for personal or accommodation-related reasons, or now that you know there is a part of your identity that you feel is worth sharing, you're ready to do so. Ultimately, sharing at work boils down to authenticity, accommodations and support, and/or setting yourself up for future success.

Navigating the accommodations process

Perhaps the biggest reason a person will disclose neurodivergence or a disability at work is because they need support or accommodations. Usually, the only way to kickstart this process of receiving modifications and adjustments to make your working life better is through disclosure.

Typically, accommodations are viewed by employers as being burdensome or worth denying from the get-go because they cause "undue hardship"—which is a fancy, legal way of saying they are too expensive or difficult to implement. This is far from the truth, with data suggesting the majority of accommodations for workers with disabilities are free for employers and cost nothing, or have a one-time price of around $300 on average (Job Accommodation Network, 2023). This is actually down from years past when the average one-time cost was higher, which goes to show how accommodation requests are usually not too difficult to approve. However, the benefits are immeasurable on top of your ability to thrive. Employers found accommodations ultimately improved interactions with coworkers, increased overall workplace morale, and increased overall company productivity (Job Accommodation Network, 2023).

But what kind of accommodations can you even request if all you know is not receiving support or that saying you are autistic is only going to open the door to a conversation or process with the folks in human resources? Depending on your work environment and type of job, you might have a ton of different options available to you. I come from law practice, where the most commonly made disability accommodations across the board for lawyers relate to changes in work tasks, scheduling, and job structure (Blanck *et al.*, 2020). You can also find ideas for accommodations at the Job Accommodation Network website (http://askjan.org)—this is also super helpful for your employer or HR representatives to browse as well, since then they can learn more about your specific disability and why certain things may prove useful for you!

The right moment to do this also is something only you can

decide on. When I spoke to Emily Shuman, the deputy director of the Rocky Mountain ADA Center for an article on disclosure for *Fast Company*, she told me that "the best thing to do is disclose that you have a disability when you realize that you cannot perform the essential functions of your job because of your disability and need an accommodation" (Moss, 2020). Disability and neurodiversity are dynamic. People can acquire neurodivergence or disability. The things you're supposed to do within your role can always change as you get promoted or take on additional responsibilities. Looking at Shuman's take, it's important to boil down the legalese on "essential functions" and understand that these are the important day-to-day responsibilities and duties you have to do in that specific job you were hired to do. If you aren't sure what the "essential functions" are, find a job description or posting for your specific job online or in the company's materials, or a description for a similar position somewhere else, and see what they say the people do each day or what they're expected to be able to do. If, despite being qualified to them, your disability makes those things harder, that's when conventional wisdom says you should disclose and request an accommodation if you haven't already done so.

The best example I can give of this is if you are working in a library. Think of what people who work in libraries do: they restock books, sign people up for library cards, help people borrow and check out books to bring home, and point you to which shelves and sections hold which types of books; some are also pros at knowing how to conduct research and find and use credible sources. One of your restocking duties is to lift and carry books each day to put back on the shelves—and some of them are really heavy or add up when you have stacks of them!

Let's pretend you were in an accident, unrelated to work, that temporarily makes it so you can no longer lift those books by yourself. That doesn't mean you're a bad librarian or unable to work in the library anymore. It means you probably need some help in the form of an accommodation such as using a cart to transport the books back from the circulation desk and back onto the shelves, or having someone else to help you carry and reshelve the books. You'd probably tell your boss about your injury and that you need an accommodation to help you bring the books back to the shelves. Together, you'd brainstorm whether or not the cart, a break from shelving books, or having a coworker help you might be the best solution. They can't decide you are no longer allowed to work in the library, nor does it make it okay if they start bullying you for wearing a cast on your arm to the point you no longer feel comfortable showing up to your shift at the library. And how you go about this would be up to you. Maybe all you share is that you were recently injured and it's best not to aggravate the pain. Maybe you have a doctor's note or report sharing that you shouldn't lift heavy objects as part of the healing process, and you choose to share that. Or maybe you have a good enough relationship that you tell the story of what happened and why you need help. All of this is an exercise in practicing self-advocacy in order to achieve your goal of getting an accommodation so you can do your job to the best of your ability.

Dealing with ableist colleagues who know you're neurodivergent

Not everyone you encounter is going to be super accepting, unfortunately. Dealing with ableist attitudes at work is a possibility, and depending on the severity of an unaccepting person's conduct, you might have options. Maybe someone makes an offhand joke or comment that doesn't sit well with you. Maybe someone is making fun of you behind your back. Or you're simply not getting the same assignments and responsibilities as someone else in the exact same role, and you suspect a disability is the reason.

It's natural to be quick to jump to the history of how neurodivergent people are often bullied and excluded from the time we are children to explain bad workplace behavior. However, workplace bullying isn't as widespread as you'd expect. A 2012 study reported one-third of autistic employees experienced bullying or harassment at work, while a 2009 report from the U.S. Department of Education found more than 88 percent of young people with autism reported being treated "pretty well" at work (Hensel, 2017). Compared to the amount of us who are bullied as children and teenagers, this is really promising stuff—assuming we are people who know we are autistic and successfully land jobs in the first place. Keep in mind that the number of autistic people at work will always be higher than the numbers that these surveys poll due to those who do not disclose or do not know they are neurodivergent to begin with.

But workplace bullying or harassment at work can be subtle. Social bullying and other forms of exclusion may be more prevalent when people are not understanding of differences associated with autism. Sometimes in these instances of ableism, disclosure and a good conversation to work through your feelings and differences might be of service to make your work environment more pleasant.

Harassment can also be emboldened in the remote environment, as people can feel more confident saying hurtful or ableist things when they can hide behind a screen and don't have to say it to your face. If a colleague is harassing you online (whether through official channels like email or team messaging and meeting platforms, or unofficial channels like social media), make sure to document those instances so you can report them to a trusted supervisor or human resources pro within your company to deal with the bullying accordingly. Writing things digitally works two ways—we talk about how disclosures online can live forever, but so do the hurtful things people say. That double-edged sword should allow you to prevail towards justice and psychological safety if you are bullied or harassed virtually by someone at work, whether it is a colleague or client.

Social bullying at work can be exclusion, offhand comments, or public reprimands, but those do not rise to the level of harassment (Nagele-Piazza, 2018). Exclusion at work and the occasional offhand comment can be hurtful, and you might want to talk it out with the colleague who is hurting you before taking it up with human resources or a supervisor.

If the difficulties neurodivergent employees encounter border on harassment rather than social bullying, your options for proceeding may differ. If you are being harassed, you might have legal recourse and should definitely document the incidents with human resources or supervisors and managers. Harassment based on autism or disability is a form of discrimination. The U.S. Equal Employment Opportunity Commission (EEOC)'s webpage on disability discrimination explains:

> Although the law doesn't prohibit simple teasing, offhand comments, or isolated incidents that are not very serious, harassment is illegal when it is so frequent or severe that it creates a hostile or offensive work environment or when it

results in an adverse employment decision (such as being fired or demoted).

These instances of harassment and discrimination may invoke civil rights laws such as the Americans with Disabilities Act, where harassment and other forms of discrimination are prohibited and you are protected against them.

I hate saying that change falls on neurodivergent people, but finding trusted allies and working to build change towards a positive and accepting workplace culture is an option you have towards combating ableism. You might want to offer to lead or bring in speakers or facilitators for your company to have anti-ableism and neurodiversity trainings so everybody, not just the perceived or confirmed bullies and exclusionary people, can learn to accept and treat everyone better. As someone who leads disability and neurodiversity trainings, I promise they don't just benefit nondisabled, neurotypical people—they lead to lightbulb moments for people who have neurodivergent and disabled family members, or suspect they might be neurodivergent themselves.

Employee resource groups and related disability inclusion initiatives

Another option for support at work and finding like-minded people is through affinity groups. If your company is large enough, you probably have what are known as employee resource groups (ERGs) or business affinity groups. ERGs are groups of people who join forces around a shared characteristic or identity, like race, gender, sexual orientation, or disability. They are usually overseen by human resources or diversity, equity, and inclusion professionals who work for your organization, but the individual group leaders are your fellow employees and colleagues. Disability and/or neurodiversity employee resources are often made up of neurodivergent people, parents, siblings, allies, and others who simply want to learn more and do better. They have the potential to help new hires feel welcomed, provide mentorship, and increase diversity in the workplace (Goode, 2016). Having a group of people band together over something like disability and neurodiversity can bring invaluable perspective to your workplace. This strength in numbers and "not only you" approach can ensure the workplace represents employees with disabilities and provides support. Employee resource groups also better the company by bringing in outside speakers, presenters, and trainings on diversity and inclusion issues relating to the theme of the group—this is a way to bring in awesome education without one person feeling responsible or as if they're undertaking a massive burden by advocating for their own safety and inclusion.

Sometimes disclosing can put you in the position where you become the "go-to" person for all neurodiversity- and disability-related information within the company, or the "spokesperson" for all neurodivergent people. When this happens, you might feel nervous. You may feel the spokesperson phenomenon is showing up if you are one of several openly neurodivergent employees (maybe even the only openly neurodivergent one) expected to take on an ERG leadership role, create an ERG, or lead trainings and become the workplace neurodiversity spokesperson. Companies are taking diversity, equity, and inclusion initiatives and strategies seriously, and might view your openness as an asset that benefits their bottom line. Wanting or needing support in the workplace does not mean you have to be a voice for everyone who has a disability or is neurodivergent in your workplace or community; ideally, your voice is one of many in the conversation. This is a valid concern to have, but it should not stop you from seeking support.

Some people are happy to get more involved in disability advocacy, and being thrust into this "spokesperson" role can be a great way to blend your passion with your professional role. Some of my best colleagues have anonymously run large social media accounts but privately worked to make inclusion better in large companies and kept the public and private personas separate; their passions would shine in both realms, and if they ever decided to give up the anonymity, it would continue to make an impact. I meet a lot of young disabled and neurodivergent people who do want to get involved in advocacy, and if you are being thrust into a spokesperson role at work, it can be a great place to start if that's one of your goals. Of course, there is no pressure, and your needs and desires come first—you do not have to agree to lead a neurodiversity training, join an employee resource group, or be everyone's point person for personal questions. It can be overwhelming and a lot of (often) unpaid additional responsibility and labor that's outside your usual job duties. If you feel this way, be sure to set appropriate boundaries with your managers and company leaders who are leading the diversity strategy, and politely and professionally decline (you can do this over email). You can always change your mind down the road, but remember, communication is key and don't feel obligated or pressured into disclosing more than you feel comfortable with. Enforce your boundaries and protect your peace so you can continue to have career satisfaction.

If you suspect you are being discriminated against

If you do suspect you've been a victim of harassment, bullying, discrimination, or retaliation at work, you have a few options.

The first is to look at your employee handbook. Chances are, there is an anti-harassment policy or some kind of Equal Employment Opportunity policy that makes clear the type of behavior that is prohibited under most major civil rights laws based on protected characteristics, like race and gender, but also possibly including disability. Under those policies, there is usually a complaints procedure, and your workplace can't retaliate and treat you worse or differently because you chose to follow that procedure (i.e., they can't decide to pass you over for a promotion because you were "difficult" and complained about a denied accommodation or workplace bullying).

As for denial of accommodations, I always recommend you put all requests for accommodations in writing—even after you've had an in-person or phone conversation. If we verbally agree on an accommodation, I send a follow-up email recapping what we talked about and that accommodation's implementation, so there is a record of the conversation that holds everyone accountable and there is some kind of proof if things don't go as planned. If your accommodation is denied, ask if there is an appeals process and also for the reasoning and rationale (in writing, preferably) for *why* your accommodation was denied. You can go from there in trying to escalate the situation internally or decide whether it is best to involve a legal course of action.

Reacting as an employer: what to do when someone discloses a disability or you suspect one

I am so lucky that, most days, I get to talk to corporate leaders who genuinely want to make employment and the workplace a better fit for neurodivergent people. Sometimes, it turns out, these dedicated champions are there because someone they know and love is neurodivergent or disabled, or they are themselves. Typically, there are a few things managers and employers can do to make the disclosure journey go a little more smoothly based on how they react to this new information.

Listen closely

Disclosure can happen at any time or place, planned or spontaneous. It can be at a diversity and inclusion meeting, a one-off comment about a disability, or in an HR meeting. It can also be unplanned as a way to explain behavior or why something wasn't turned in on time or why someone reacted a certain way in a specific situation (Moss, 2020). First and foremost, try to figure out *why* this information is being shared with you—is it to request support and accommodation, to explain what's been going on with the person's performance, or because they simply want to share with you? The time, manner, demeanor, and context are all clues you can use to determine someone's intent, as well as directly asking them.

Don't be judgmental

Judgment catches us off guard (even if we think we are mentally prepared for it). That judgment often takes the form of additional questions or seemingly well-intentioned microaggressions.

Some of the most frustrating things that I've heard when explaining my disability to an employer are comments like "But you don't look autistic," "I never would have guessed if you didn't tell me," or making a comparison between my autism and that of another autistic person, saying I am "higher-functioning." This is a common experience for many people with "invisible" disabilities that have a degree of passing or masking involved. Not everyone feels comfortable with follow-up questions or is willing to provide additional information beyond that initial disclosure or seeking of support.

Disclosure at work often requires planning, self-advocacy, and bracing ourselves for any and all types of reaction. A microaggression or judgmental response can put someone in an uncomfortable position. You have a split second usually to decide whether to ignore the feeling of hurt or to advocate for yourself more forcefully. For instance, after introducing myself to a new colleague, they told me how inspirational my story was and how they'd never have guessed I was autistic. I felt like I had to smile and thank them, despite their ableist remarks; with a friend, I might tell them all about the concept of inspiration porn and Stella Young's groundbreaking 2014 TEDx Talk and why I often do not feel "inspiration" is a kind compliment.

In contrast, if you respond in a positive, nonjudgmental way, that allows me to share freely. The easiest ways to do this are saying things like "Thank you so much for telling me," in order to affirm trust, or "I'm glad you shared that with me," or using language that feels genuine and natural to explicitly convey empathy or admit that maybe this additional information explained helped you better understand us (sort of an alignment with the double empathy problem, if you may).

Offer support, if appropriate

One of the most common questions I get asked is by managers who actually are a lot more perceptive and knowledgeable than I anticipate. They know neurodivergent and disabled people, and they know a lot of the shared traits and characteristics to the point that they recognize and perceive neurodivergence in people they are working with and supervising, who have never uttered a word about it or disclosed a disability. A lot of the time, it feels apparent in some way these people don't know or need support in order to be more successful, more productive, more…something that's lacking in how we measure workplace performance.

"I suspect my colleague is neurodivergent," a manager will ask me. *"Should I bring it up with them?"*

Every time someone asks me this, my answer is typically no. While it's a great question, and I know personally I have a very good instinct and sense of who is and isn't neurodivergent (even if the person I know has no clue about their own brain), it isn't always my place to say something. I am not a therapist, and chances are, neither are you. It is not my place to tell my employees or people I work with what to do about their neurology, health, or wellbeing, or force them into disclosing information they don't already know or feel comfortable sharing with me for whatever reason.

However, you can gently push someone into what I consider

a *soft disclosure* when you can neither confirm nor deny someone has a disability. You might notice the metrics where an employee who likely is neurodivergent is falling short and failing to measure up, and you, being the great team leader you are, want to course correct and make sure this person keeps their job and succeeds. You're going to look at this person's traits and metrics as objectively as possible. Are they showing up late more often than usual? Are they sluggish? Irritable? See what seems to be the contributing factors to them not being up to par. I consider this a soft disclosure since neurodiversity or a nonapparent disability might not be the reason behind a recurring pattern or a new change in workplace behavior and output, but someone can give context or some kind of clue as to how you can help them or set up some safeguards or support. I know I am sluggish and irritable if I don't get enough sleep, and some people are this way after a death in the family or a major personal situation that they don't feel up to talking about, so if you mention something such as "I notice you haven't been yourself lately; you seemed a little upset in our last meeting. Is everything okay?"—and you have a very strong hunch that it isn't—this can be a great jumping-off point for someone to share if there's a taxing situation at home, to admit they haven't been themselves, or to disclose. When or if they do, you are ready to go as an empathetic listener who can point them in the direction of resources or make tweaks and modifications to help them succeed at their job. You might also choose to review some of this stuff with someone who reports to you at their annual review and discuss how you can help them improve in a nonjudgmental, supportive way.

If someone is hesitant to open up, don't be afraid to respond with some vulnerability of your own and establish yourself as a point person, equal, and ally. "I mean, I had a really crappy day"—then share something semi-specific and follow up—"No really, how are you?" If you have that kind of relationship, it shows you are leading with trust rather than forcing someone to trust you.

The exception to this answer being a straight-up no is when it's my close friends or someone I have a really good and trusted rapport with. I might be more likely to say, "Hey, I've noticed we do a lot of the same things," and share a little bit more of the common characteristics and traits that align with autism—"Is there any chance you might also be autistic?"—and I'll do it in such a way it's light but somewhat serious so they don't take offense, or don't feel like they were hiding something if they originally elected not to tell me for whatever reason (this has happened with many a colleague, who has told me they had ADHD well after we began working together and then I'd instinctively say, "That explains why we do some of the same things and get along so well," due to the overlap and similarities between autism and ADHD). In these cases, it's liberating and creates a closeness. With a stranger, though, it can feel like an absolute invasion of privacy or a personal attack of sorts.

CHAPTER 8

DISCLOSING FOR INDIVIDUALS
Random Situations Where You May Self-Advocate and Disclose

S OME OF THESE SITUATIONS were discussed in the contexts of children, and how family members and others may handle the situation—but what if you're an adult, or you're practicing your self-advocacy skills and on your own personal journey towards feeling empowered or practicing self-advocacy in public? These are some of the random situations in life that crop up where disclosure might be unexpected, welcomed, or either more spontaneous or deliberate compared to sharing with your family, friends, romantic partners, or workplace colleagues.

Advocating in public and with strangers

I talk to people I don't know very well about my autism almost daily, but it's very different because they are strangers I meet through work, and I know my responsibility at events and the services my business provides are to educate the public on autism, neurodiversity, and disability. Telling my story is a key part of that.

However, I don't disclose when it is unnecessary or feels like a potential invasion of my privacy. This can be as seemingly benign and a one-off situation as a viral video, but other times it can permeate throughout everyday life. I take rideshares almost daily because I do not have a car, nor do I wish to drive in a major city or rent a car when I travel for work. I come into contact with strangers driving me places every day, and I never see the need to disclose my autism out of necessity or just to make conversation during the ride. I have only felt it relevant once to disclose because I once had a rideshare driver who mentioned she was working towards her master's degree to help autistic kids, and I asked her how she had become interested—apparently, I sounded too knowledgeable, so I felt inclined to disclose. It was a lovely half-hour conversation, and we parted ways. It's not a decision I often think about making during these little moments, but other moments throughout my day, my autism feels as if it takes center stage and I am sharing or reminding people I am autistic through my social media presence, or possibly in other situations like airports, sporting events, or doctor's appointments.

Sharing on the internet

When it comes to talking about neurodiversity on the internet, I typically worry about oversharing. I think about people who forget that the internet is not written in pencil but in ink.

However, for neurodivergent people, social media, blogs, and videos are one of many ways in which we connect, relate, and understand our experiences. I first began sharing my story offline and began sharing artwork and charity-related things online only. It wasn't until I was officially a published author for the first time at 16 years old and had news coverage about me that I considered saying I was autistic on the internet. After all, when CNN and your local newspapers already did it for you, you might as well own your story on your own terms. It has since meant you cannot Google my name without learning I am autistic, so it is an open secret at best and a consistent, readily available disclosure with anyone I meet at worst (though thankfully, not everyone feels compelled to Google everyone they come into contact with). I do not regret any of that, as neurodiversity advocacy has been my passion for well over half of my life now, but if my interests had changed or I wanted to distance myself from being proudly autistic everywhere, I'd have very different thoughts. Sharing in a one-off post to receive support or tell a story is very different from the majority of your posts, memes, and everything in between being autism, neurodiversity, or disability adjacent.

I will admit I follow an unwieldy number of autism and neurodiversity meme pages and creators, often laughing, smiling, wincing, or sharing them with friends with the thought "This explains me better than I can explain me!" Content is a language that everyone speaks fluently, it seems. I do not consider myself a content creator but a content consumer.

Your content consumption habits can inadvertently be a disclosure; if someone goes through the list of people and accounts you follow, the sheer number of meme pages can say you're neurodivergent. If you're nervous about this among your peer group or others, you can always make another account just to keep all of your neurodiversity stuff separate, and seek support or share your own story under an alias. That way, your "real-world" identity is safe, and you aren't saying more than you'd like to out in the open.

If you're a creator or want to create, that's awesome! Again, consider what you're sharing—try your best to be authentic to yourself in a way you feel comfortable with, disclose as you please, and consider the benefits and consequences for your personal and professional situation. Having boundaries, your own voice, and maybe a dash of humor or stark realism can go a long way. A lot of us want to educate and help others, and become a source of inspiration, a resource, or end up building community for others. All of this, along with managing your personal story, can become a huge responsibility.

On the road again: disclosing while traveling

I didn't take an airplane by myself until I was 21 years old, going to visit somebody over spring break in Washington, D.C. I didn't prepare anything ahead of time other than to pack my luggage for my trip in compliance with airport security measures and rules. I was very nervous as I took my shoes off and sent my belongings through the security scanner. Everything felt very loud and crowded. I had heard horror stories of stimming and other autistic traits and behaviors being viewed as suspicious by security staff and dreaded the idea of being detained or touched by a stranger in an additional screening. I must have looked as anxious as I felt because the woman in front of me waited for me to collect my belongings, said she had a child my age, and pointed me in the right direction of the gate I was heading to.

I've traveled plenty since that first trip to Washington. Since then, I've registered for TSA Pre-Check so I don't have to feel my feet on the cold hard floors at an American airport from removing my shoes. I pack fairly lightly and have had kind and respectful interactions with agents and officers who selected me for additional screenings. Sure, I find it all a little overwhelming, but generally not to the point it's too much or I say I'm autistic, because now I am a seasoned pro.

The last time I felt that anxiety creep in was on an international business trip to Canada, and I had to interact with customs officers on both the Canadian and American side, as well as face different rules for security screenings in Canada (while I didn't disclose, the security officer was very kind when she informed me that my toothpaste tube was too large per Canadian regulations and reassured me that I wasn't in trouble when she confiscated it) before sending me off to pre-clear customs before coming back home. I don't think disclosure would've helped, but looking back, I do think for autistic travelers going abroad, it might be helpful to look at a country's regulations and have an idea of what a customs or immigration officer may ask, in order to feel safe and prepared, as well as decide whether or not a disclosure is appropriate—in my experience, it wasn't since I was only asked the purpose of my visit and how long I would be staying on entry, and on return I was only asked what I was bringing back into the country to make sure I didn't have any prohibited items. My autism was irrelevant there, but had they harassed me or wrongly accused me or made me believe I did something wrong, I possibly could have frozen up or had a meltdown that prompted further explanation since I was traveling solo, and no one was there to advocate alongside me.

I have since learned that disclosing autism could potentially make it easier or make the journey go more smoothly for many other autistic people. When disclosing disability to airlines, they have to make sure to uphold your civil rights, but they can also accommodate you by allowing you to travel with an emotional support animal, pre-board a plane, or offer other forms of assistance to make your journey feel less turbulent.

Access and assistance when traveling as an individual with a disability

In the U.S., you can sign up with *TSA Cares* to receive accommodations during the security screening process. Disclosing at the screening process might make it so officers are less likely to select your autistic loved one for additional screening because they think stimming, pacing, or other neurodivergent behaviors are "suspicious." Some airports allow you to schedule a practice run if you disclose, so the real thing is less stressful and overwhelming. Disclosing that you have a disability like autism can also allow you and/or your family to fly with a service animal or an emotional support animal, if you have one. It can also allow you to pre-board a plane when it is less crowded and time-consuming. If you are denied accommodations based on autism that is disclosed to the airline or airport, be sure to check your state and country's civil rights laws and practices to file a complaint.

Other options include things like the *Hidden Disabilities Sunflower* lanyards and bracelets, which are a discrete way to disclose and are recognized at airports and entry points all around the globe. I mentioned this earlier as being a good tool for families especially, but if you're a self-advocate and don't want to share too much but feel that a wristband or lanyard would be helpful for you, this might be worth exploring. Of course, you don't have to signal you have a disability if you don't want to, and dependent on where in the world you are on any given day, the outcome may depend on how prepared airport, airline, and other staff are to help and assist you as needed.

One thing I'm noticing more and more of is *quiet and sensory rooms* at stadiums and airports. I've never personally used them, but I do appreciate a quiet space that doesn't involve running into a nearby bathroom to escape the crowds, find some privacy, or recollect my thoughts when I'm scared or overwhelmed (how many of us have done that at an event or public place before?). Having gone to enough sporting events with tens of thousands of people, I only wished quiet and sensory rooms had existed earlier in my life. They would've meant my best friend and I wouldn't be leaving basketball games early because I couldn't handle the squeaking shoes. If sports or airports are part of your itinerary, they can become instantly less terrible.

While it can feel scary to request a dry run or special assistance, something I've learned about making travel more accessible is *you are not taking away from someone else's experience if you have a genuine access need.* This circles back to my own internalized ableism. Theme parks in particular have programs to assist guests with disabilities so they can more easily access attractions without having to wait in crowded, noisy queues to go on rides or meet their favorite characters. Disney in particular is especially great with their Disability Access Service. I am an adrenaline seeker and love roller coasters, but the screaming children in hour-long lines are enough to send me into a sensory overload or potential meltdown; this fact alone makes disability services super helpful for me. But as a young adult, I was hesitant to request these types of accommodations because I can (although with great difficulty) brave the long lines to ride my favorite rides—I didn't think I "needed" it as much as say, an autistic six-year-old might who does not have the same advocacy and coping skills. I was afraid my own needs would make it so the child's needs wouldn't be met. However, access is for everyone—not just the young or the elderly. That same child might be in line with me regardless, and hopefully the adults in their life have the resources and skills to advocate for them to have a more inclusive vacation as well. There is no shame in needing or requesting help. After all, vacations in particular are supposed to be fun and enjoyable—not stressful and inaccessible!

Gyms, fitness, and recreational activities

I am a self-proclaimed couch potato and a proud member of the club of kids who were picked last in gym class to be on any team. I was so athletically inclined as a teenager that when I signed up for my high school's rowing training camp in order to possibly join the team in my freshman year, I famously passed out on the first day we went on the water and did not finish the training camp. However, as I get older, I have become more involved with the fitness community by joining a gym after years of experimentation to find a routine that works for me. I am not particularly good at working out—I don't run, but I am trying to stay motivated, not hurt myself, and gain some ancillary health benefits like a clearer head and better-quality sleep.

A lot of gyms and health clubs, however, can be sensory nightmares. There are bright lights, lots of people, various types of equipment, and loud music in group classes. Autistics' first brush with physical activity might be to improve motor skills. If dexterity and motor skills related to an activity are a concern, it might be helpful to bring that up to a trainer, staff member, or instructor in order to make sure they offer an alternative so you don't end up injuring yourself or feeling excluded. Often at fitness centers, instructors and trainers make a callout before a class or activity to let them know if you have any physical limitations or injuries that they should know about so they can modify exercises for you. This would be a good time to disclose a chronic illness, physical disability, or other motor skills limitation, especially as it relates to your personal safety. You can also arrive early to meet the leaders, coaches, or others to disclose and see if they can help you in some way. I don't usually do this, but I have considered it since I lack spatial awareness sometimes and don't know where all my body parts are in space (i.e., when there is a cue to have a flat back, I have no idea if I am hunched over too much or if my back is flat)—that way, the instructor can keep an eye out to make sure I don't injure myself. This is when I consider disclosure a winning situation—it has a literal health benefit or the potential to avoid a negative consequence. You might also disclose in order to make the space more accommodating, such as asking if the music can be turned down a notch to a slightly more reasonable level to be more inclusive or if they provide earplugs to help minimize the sound.

Others purposely build community spaces and activities

for neurodivergent and disabled people, such as sports offerings through programs like Special Olympics or independent studios and instructors wanting to create sensory-friendly, accessible spaces. When I wrote about how fitness can be overwhelming for a Greatist column, I spoke to Mikhaela Ackerman, an autistic yoga instructor, who explained how strong scents and heat might not be accessible; when she teaches neurodivergent students, she tries to use low lighting and incorporate weighted blankets into the exercises to create a joyful, relaxing, and stimulating form of movement (Moss, 2019a). Something about this sat well with me—that disabled people really do belong everywhere and anywhere, and with the right allies in the right places, we can have activities previously thought to only be for a certain type of people or athletes to truly be inclusive of all of us.

If you're wanting to get in shape or be a part of recreational activities that are designed to be wholly inclusive, check out your municipality's parks and recreation department or activities. When I was on my city's disability affairs citizen's advisory board, we knew the city held various social clubs, activities, and programs for people with disabilities, as well as their caregivers and families, to participate in. Sometimes, you need people who get it, rather than having to seek an accommodation in an environment that might never be accessible for you no matter how hard you try, because it's unfortunately not in the activity's DNA to be inclusive (I cannot imagine a silent workout class; instead of loud music, I'd hear people's feet pounding on a treadmill and would prefer the music to nod along to).

Higher education: disclosing at college, university, and post-secondary programs

Possibly the thing with the highest level of anticipation that can happen in the disclosure realm is becoming a legal adult. Nowhere does this show up as much as if you are planning on continuing your studies and enrolling in any form of higher education, like a college or university. While colleges and universities do have plenty of supports available for students with disabilities, it is a place you're often expected to advocate for yourself without any support. If your parents or guardians try to do it for you, they'll likely be ignored or dismissed because you are an adult and your academic records and health information are yours, even if you've consented. When I was transitioning to college, my parents were able to help me in the disclosure and advocacy process only because I was 17 years old—a minor, and therefore not an adult and not already on campus and taking classes. Once I was 18, it was just me out there. Higher education is traditionally exclusionary of neurodivergent students, failing to meet our needs and rife with institutional ableism. Due to social and academic challenges, autistic students historically face lower levels of degree completion (Bakker *et al.*, 2023).

To assist with disclosure, start with your college or university's *disability services office*. You can usually visit them in person when you're on campus, or see what information they have posted online about registering or making an appointment. Disclosure usually happens when you meet with a human or fill out some forms. Everyone there has experience working with disabled and neurodivergent students. These are the people who can help you get academic and university-related accommodations. You might need to bring information related to your diagnosis to them so they can verify you have a disability, such as medical records or previous records of accommodations from your primary and secondary school years. If not, they might be able to point you in the right direction for an assessment to determine your eligibility for disability and accessibility services.

Typically, disability services in higher education will offer neurodivergent students extra time on exams or note-taking services, but if you know there are other things you struggle with or need help with, start by bringing up those challenges and work towards a solution together. I never knew I could ask for things that weren't extra time. I didn't know note-taking services would be beneficial for me, nor did I know I was eligible for them, so I never asked. Looking back, that would've made my time in higher education a lot less stressful since I often couldn't decipher what was important in a lecture and what wasn't, and write it down or type it out fast enough—let alone the fact I could be easily distracted if I had my laptop open or by another student's behavior or mannerisms in class.

One form of advocacy that disability services do well (in my opinion) is advocating to professors and instructors, especially if you go to a large university where you might not get to interact with your professor one-on-one all that much or if the professors refuse to grant accommodations that students with disabilities are entitled to. The institution's ADA coordinators, as well as disability and access services, have resources and influence within the university bureaucracy that students often do not, so they can make things happen for you.

When it comes to disclosing to professors, that's also a personal choice. I rarely did it except for one time in law school when I had a very visibly bad day. I was unprepared, which was wholly out of character for me, and actually began crying after class and apologizing profusely. I ended up telling my professor I had a meltdown related to my autism, and she was incredibly supportive and told me I could have an opportunity to present to the class another day when I felt calm and prepared.

Another resource available to you is likely your university's counseling center. Most offer free or low-cost mental health services to students, which can be a huge relief. However, whether or not the providers are neurodiversity affirming or understanding is a whole other story, and this may or may not be helpful to you.

Sharing: healthcare decisions and doctors

One of the worst disclosure situations I've been in was when I was at my university's student health center. I disclosed my autism after the physician's assistant asked if I had any pre-existing conditions. Then I watched the physician's assistant note in my chart that autism "was something I had in childhood," which is an inaccurate characterization of autism. With uneven knowledge bases among providers and misinformation ending up in my chart, I realized advocating for my healthcare needs that day became even more of an uphill battle than if I stayed quiet. It took more than one follow-up visit to receive the care I had been advocating for and requested at the time because the physician assistant didn't listen to me or perceive me as competent after making that notation. These biases are pervasive in healthcare. In an article for NPR about disabled healthcare biases, Angel Miles, a Black woman who is a wheelchair user, explained: "I'm often ignored... I'm often spoken at, and not to" (Shapiro, 2020). I couldn't have echoed that sentiment more when I would advocate for a solution only to be disregarded, or if I brought a support person and they brought up the exact same thing—it would sometimes be the only way my concern was taken seriously.

Despite poor experiences in the past, I typically disclose to healthcare professionals regardless of whether it is relevant to medical treatment because I request a specific accommodation—you, as the professional, explain things to me in a way I can understand and let me know what you are going to be doing (i.e., please *actually* tell me if I am getting a vaccine and when and where you are going to be injecting me since I have zero intention of looking and want to be mentally prepared, or if you are planning to use your hands to touch certain parts of my body that may be more sensitive and lead to a potentially unwanted sensory experience so I can give informed consent). I have left physician's practices before over denying this simple request or feeling as if a boundary I was setting was being violated for non-emergency, routine checkups and examinations.

I also like to bring a support person as an accommodation to appointments—usually my mom—just in case I forget something important or understate its importance. I think a lot of neurotypical and nondisabled people do this for various medical appointments, such as fertility-related, surgical, and cancer-related appointments where it helps to have a relative or supporter present to ask questions because it's scary or concerns multiple parties. Sometimes nondisabled people do this in order to make decisions if the patient is unable to consent or give feedback of any kind because they are unwell or under anesthesia. However, bringing a support person as a neurodivergent individual (and sharing I am neurodivergent) means I have to be vocal if the doctor starts talking to my support person as if I am not in the room—in which case I have either prepped my mom to prompt me to answer, or I'll just start talking and answering the doctor's question on my own, without missing a beat. If it continues to happen to the point where I am feeling very uncomfortable, I might say something or consider finding a new provider.

Conclusion

THERE IS A LOT OF DISCLOSURE ground covered throughout this book, and realizing just how complex and messy the journey and each individual situation can be is part of the human side of telling your story. Since it's a lot of information and sometimes all at once, I want to leave you with a few notes and thoughts before sending you back out into the world.

- Be informed (or continue to educate yourself) on information relating to a disability or forms of neurodivergence you identify with. That way, you'll have a good jumping-off point for your discussions. This can include medical definitions, current pop culture representations and discussions, and language to use.

- Treat disclosure and advocacy like putting together a toolbox. Your strategy, whether you're a family member or self-advocate, will depend on the situation. Remember, all disclosure ultimately comes down to seeking support, accommodations, and/or acceptance. What tools in your toolbox will you be using to get there?

- Part of that toolbox involves going back to the basics of storytelling— who, what, where, why, and how. You already have a "what"—you're talking the talk! Possibly the most important of these is figuring out your "why" for disclosing, then you can work backwards on who to tell, where and when is appropriate, and how to develop or choose the best strategy to share.

- It is okay to need time, space, and practice. Perfect tools won't magically appear in the toolbox overnight. Sometimes they require crafting, refining, time away, reflection, and a new perspective. You will always feel like you're practicing, until one day you have more confidence and recognize you've got this!

- Resources of all types can be valid for assistance in explaining yourself and communicating. Do not underestimate the power of a book or article that explains your experiences, or even a simple meme, image, or video that somehow has the perfect words or gives you a "this is what it feels like to be me" reaction in a way other people will understand.

- Remember, if someone else reacts negatively or treats you differently (and not in a good way) after you disclose, that is most likely not your fault. It's easy to think you did something wrong or feel a sense of regret, but chances are it is a lot of information for a neurotypical person or potential new ally to process, and they don't always know what to do, either. Unless they say something outwardly mean and rude, try to assume good intentions and that they, too, are learning and want to "get it right" but might not be sure how.

- The right people won't always have the right words or know the perfect solutions to offer support or accommodations, but they will always somehow have a way of reassuring you that they are accepting.

Disclosure and conversations about disability and autism are lifelong and evolve with each and every relationship; we spend a lifetime disclosing and discovering new and important things worth sharing about ourselves and our communities. I am still learning, too, and I am excited about where this journey takes us. Sometimes disclosure won't always go the way we planned every single time, but hopefully, as time goes on, it will get easier.

References

American Psychiatric Association (APA) (2013) *Diagnostical and Statistical Manual of Mental Disorders, Fifth Edition: DSM-5*. Washington, DC: APA.

Autism Speaks (2024) "Bullying Facts & Figures." www.autismspeaks.org/bullying-facts-figures

Autistic Self Advocacy Network (2024) "About Autism." https://autisticadvocacy.org/about-asan/about-autism

Bågenholm, A. and Gillberg, C. (1991) "Psychosocial effects on siblings of children with autism and mental retardation: A population-based study." *Journal of Intellectual Disability Research 35*, 4, 291–307. https://doi.org/10.1111/j.1365-2788.1991.tb00403.x

Bakker, Theo, Krabbendam, Lydia, Bhulai, Sandjaj, Meeter, Martijn, and Begeer, Sander (2023) "Study progression and degree completion of autistic students in higher education: A longitudinal study." *Higher Education 85*, 1–26. https://doi.org/10.1007/s10734-021-00809-1

Blanck, Peter, Abdul-Malak, Ynesse, Adya, Meera, Hyseni, Fitore, Killeen, Mary, and Altunkol Wise, Fatma (2020) "Diversity and Inclusion in the American Legal Profession: First Phase Findings from a National Study of Lawyers with Disabilities and Lawyers Who Identify as LGBTQ+." *University of the District of Columbia Law Review 23*, 1, 3. https://digitalcommons.law.udc.edu/udclr/vol23/iss1/3

Bologna, Caroline (2021, March 4) "How to Talk to Your Kid About Disabilities." HuffPost. www.huffpost.com/entry/how-to-talk-to-kids-disabilities_l_603 68650c5b6dfb6a735d8b4

Centers for Disease Control and Prevention (2023, April 4) "Data & Statistics on Autism Spectrum Disorder." www.cdc.gov/ncbddd/autism/data.html

Center for Disability Rights (n.d.) "#Ableism." https://cdrnys.org/blog/uncategorized/ableism

Connolly, Ciaran (2014, September 10) "61% Of Autistic Children are Bullied at School in the United Kingdom, NoBullying Discovers Why." www.prweb.com/releases/61_of_autistic_children_are_bullied_at_school_in_the_united_kingdom_nobullying_discovers_why/prweb12150271.htm

Crossley, Mary (2017) "Ending-Life Decisions: Some Disability Perspectives." *Georgia State University Law Review 33*, 4, 893. https://readingroom.law.gsu.edu/gsulr/vol33/iss4/2

EEOC (n.d.) "Disability Discrimination and Employment Decisions." U.S. Equal Employment Opportunity Commission. www.eeoc.gov/disability-discrimination-and-employment-decisions

Flaherty, Catherine (2014) *Autism: What Does It Mean to Me?* Future Horizons.

Goode, Shelton (2016) "Are Employee Resource Groups Good For Business?" SHRM. www.shrm.org/topics-tools/news/hr-magazine/employee-resource-groups-good-business

Greenfest, Sara (2016, May 12) "6 Things Students with Learning Disabilities Are Tired of Hearing." Teen Vogue. www.teenvogue.com/gallery/learning-disabilities-student-myths

Hensel, Wendy F. (2017) "People with Autism Spectrum Disorder in the Workplace: An Expanding Legal Frontier." *Harvard Civil Rights–Civil Liberties Law Review 52*. https://ssrn.com/abstract=2916911

Job Accommodation Network. http://askjan.org

Job Accommodation Network (2023, May 4) "Costs and Benefits of Accommodation." https://askjan.org/topics/costs.cfm

Kapp, Steven K., Steward, Robyn, Crane, Laura, Elliott, Daisy, *et al.* (2019). "'People should be allowed to do what they like': Autistic adults' views and experiences of stimming." *Autism 23*, 7, 1782–1792. https://doi.org/10.1177/1362361319829628

Kim, Cynthia (2013, June 26) "Decoding the High Functioning Label, Musings of an Aspie." https://musingsofanaspie.com/2013/06/26/decoding-the-high-functioning-label

Ladau, Emily (2015, July 20) "Why Person-First Language Doesn't Always Put the Person First." Maryland Coalition for Inclusive Education. https://mcie.org/think-inclusive/why-person-first-language-doesnt-always-put-the-person-first

Ladau, Emily (2021) *Demystifying Disability: What to Know, What to Say, and How to be an Ally*. Clarkson Potter.

Lewis, Talila A. (2022, January 1) "Working Definition of Ableism—January 2022 Update." www.talilalewis.com/blog/working-definition-of-ableism-january-2022-update

Moorehead, Joanna (2021, December 16) "'A lot fell into place': The adults who discovered they were autistic—after their child was diagnosed." *The Guardian.* www.theguardian.com/society/2021/dec/16/adults-discovered-autistic-child-diagnosed-autism

Moss, Haley (2019a) "I Love Fitness—But It Can Be Sensory Overload." Greatist. https://greatist.com/fitness/inclusivity-gyms-sensory-overload

Moss, Haley (2019b, October 17) "Hiring neurodiverse people like me can give companies a competitive advantage." *Washington Post.* www.washingtonpost.com/outlook/2019/10/17/hiring-neurodiverse-people-like-me-can-give-companies-competitive-advantage

Moss, Haley (2020a, February 24) "How I Disclose My Disability During a Job Search." Fast Company. www.fastcompany.com/90466861/how-i-disclose-my-disability-during-a-job-search

Moss, Haley (2020b, April 15) "Diverse Autistic Authors Are Changing Neurodiversity Representation in Books." We Need Diverse Books. https://diversebooks.org/diverse-autistic-authors-are-changing-neurodiversity-representation-in-books

Moss, Haley (2020c, January 31). "Parents' Oversharing Online Can Be Particularly Problematic for Autistic Kids. Here's Why." *Washington Post.* www.washingtonpost.com/lifestyle/2020/01/31/parents-online-sharing-can-be-particularly-problematic-autistic-kids-heres-why

Moss, Haley (2021) *The Young Autistic Adult's Independence Handbook. Jessica Kingsley Publishers.*

Moss, Haley (2022, March 28) "Autistic Women and Gender Diverse People Are Often Diagnosed Late—Here's Why." Well + Good. www.wellandgood.com/autistic-women-adult-diagnosis

Moss, Haley (2023, July 5) "Rethinking Guardianship: Empowering Autistic Individuals and Preserving Rights." https://autismspectrumnews.org/rethinking-guardianship-empowering-autistic-individuals-and-preserving-rights

Nagele-Piazza, Lisa (2018) "Workplace bullying and harassment: What's the difference?" Society of Human Resource Management. www.shrm.org/topics-tools/employment-law-compliance/workplace-bullying-harassment-whats-difference

National Council on Disability (2018, March) "Beyond Guardianship: Toward Alternatives That Promote Greater Self Determination." Center for Parent Information & Resources, https://ncd.gov/sites/default/files/NCD_Guardianship_Report_Accessible.pdf

Popkin, Nancy (2019, February 6) "When Should Parents Disclose Their Child's Diagnosis?" Autism Society of North Carolina. www.autismsociety-nc.org/autism-diagnosis-disclosure

Rava, Julianna, Shattuck, Paul, Rast, Jessica, and Roux, Anne (2017) "The Prevalence and Correlates of Involvement in the Criminal Justice System Among Youth on the Autism Spectrum." *Journal of Autism and Developmental Disorders 47*, 340–346. https://doi.org/10.1007/s10803-016-2958-3

Shapiro, Joseph (2020, April 15) "People with Disabilities Fear Pandemic Will Worsen Medical Biases." NPR. www.npr.org/2020/04/15/828906002/people-with-disabilities-fear-pandemic-will-worsen-medical-biases

Sipowicz, Kasper, Podlecka, Marlena, Mokros, Łukasz, Pietras, Tadeusz, and Łuczyńska, Kamila (2022) "Being an adult sibling of an individual with autism spectrum disorder may be a predictor of loneliness and depression—Preliminary findings from a cross-sectional study." *Frontiers in Psychology 13*. https://doi.org/10.3389/fpsyg.2022.915915

Steward, Robyn (2019) *The Autism-Friendly Guide to Periods*. Jessica Kinglsey Publishers.

Turnock, Alice, Langley, Kate, and Jones, Catherine R.G. (2022) "Understanding Stigma in Autism: A Narrative Review and Theoretical Model." *Autism in Adulthood 4*, 1, 76–91. https://doi.org/10.1089%2Faut.2021.0005

Young, Stella (2014) "I'm not your inspiration, thank you very much." TEDx. www.ted.com/talks/stella_young_i_m_not_your_inspiration_thank_you_very_much?language=en